Sophia B. Jones

Also by John Steckley from Rock's Mills Press

Gibbons: The Invisible Apes

Parrots: The Flock Among Us

The Memoirs of Alexander Brodie (editor)

The Names of the Wyandot

Stories for Mia

Sophia B. Jones

The First Canadian Black Woman to Become a Doctor

Her Trials and Triumphs and Those of Her Family

Rock's Mills Press
Rock's Mills, Ontario • Oakville, Ontario
2024

Published by
Rock's Mills Press
www.rocksmillspress.com

Copyright © 2024 by John Steckley.
All rights reserved. No part of this publication may be reproduced, distributed, or transmitted in any form or by any means, including photocopying, recording, or other electronic or mechanical methods, without the prior written permission of the publisher, except in the case of brief quotations embodied in critical reviews and certain other noncommercial uses permitted by copyright law. For permission requests, contact the publisher at: customer.service@rocksmillspress.com

For adoption, trade, and bulk orders, contact the publisher at:
customer.service@rocksmillspress.com

Library and Archives Canada Cataloguing in Publication data has been applied for.

This book is a work of history, and in the interest of historical accuracy and understanding it reproduces quotations and images from the time period it describes. Some of the terms and expressions are no longer used, and some are now considered offensive and derogatory.

CONTENTS

1. How I Came to Write This Book ... 9
2. Sophia's Great Grandfather, Grandfather, and Father ... 17
3. Sophia's Uncles and an Aunt ... 34
4. Sophia and Other "Firsts" ... 71
5. Sophia's Sisters and Brothers ... 96
6. Summary and Conclusions ... 111

Sophia B. Jones

CHAPTER ONE

How I Came to Write this Book

Over the last forty years, I have been learning the Black history of Canada in short, scattered steps with, until recently, no long-term direction or intent. Over the last year or so, those steps have become much longer, more like leaps in a particular direction: learning about the lives of Sophia Bethena Jones, the first Canadian-born Black female to become a doctor, and of certain other quite interesting members of her enterprising and achieving family.

A Few Short Steps Leading to This Book
Marked as 'Coloured' in the Toronto Directory

In the early 1980s, before I was hired full time at Humber College in Toronto in 1986, I was teaching a sessional course called "Multiculturalism." Looking for information concerning the Black history of Toronto to present to my class, I found in the Humber library a book first published in 1843 that was like a phone book, but had no phone numbers as there were no phones (Howell, 1843). It did, however, include names, addresses, occupations, and, if the person were African-Canadian, the word 'coloured' was written beside their name. I learned from this prejudiced singling out of one race what occupations Black workers (all of them males) had in those days. A good number worked with tobacco, as they had previously done in the southern parts of the United States when they were slaves working in the tobacco fields before they came to Canada. More than a few of them drove horse-drawn cabs, the taxis of the time. After presenting that information in my class, I wrote about this and a few other aspects of Toronto Black history that I thought that my fellow Torontonians should learn, and got the article published in a local paper, the *Etobicoke Guardian*. I wanted to teach the multiculturalism course again, and I thought that publishing this piece might help to demonstrate my knowledge and interest in the course. In the newspaper I was referred to as a Black historian. I wasn't really, but I took it as a compliment.

Where Are You From?[1]

A few years later, after I was hired to teach at Humber College full time, I became interested in the Black history of the Maritime provinces. One reason for that was that I had a Black student who was from Nova Scotia, a province that has a long Black history. He told me that people were often asking him, "Where are you from?" and he would answer "Canada." Apparently that brought no satisfaction to the typical questioner, who would too often reply, "No. Where are you *really* from?" This produced the even more frustrating answer, "Nova Scotia." The questioners often walked away unhappy with my student's lack of a 'proper answer': e.g., Jamaica, Haiti, or somewhere else in the Caribbean, maybe even some country in Africa, somewhere 'foreign' at least. It was quite likely that his family had been living in Canada much longer than most if not all of the families of the questioners.

Learning Black History as an Editor

Some years later, I was the co-editor for Pearson Education of a doctoral dissertation written by a young African American scholar, Harvey Amani Whitfield. His manuscript told the fascinating story of Black runaway slaves from the U.S. who had settled in Nova Scotia and New Brunswick during and just after the War of 1812. The British government had issued an invitation to these people, having abolished the slave trade in 1807 and needing them as settlers for its own political purposes. The book is entitled *From American Slaves to Canadian Subjects: The Case of the Black Refugees 1813–1840* (Whitfield, 2004). It is informative and well worth reading.

Whitfield would write or edit three more books on the subject (see references below), was hired as a Professor of Black North American History at the University of Calgary, and is generally considered as a leading authority on Black slavery in the Maritime provinces. I think of him as one of my teachers on the subject of Black history in Canada

Viola Desmond

On January 25, 2015, the year of my retirement from Humber, I wrote an article for our union newsletter entitled "Black Canadian History Month—Eh?" I talked about how often during that month we heard and read about Black Americans, not Black Canadians. I included a short discussion of Vi-

---

1. This is the title of Gillian Creese's 2020 book, *"Where Are You From?" Growing Up African-Canadian in Vancouver.*

ola Desmond (1914–1965), who, in 1946, paid extra money to see a movie in Nova Scotia and sat in a seat on the theatre's main floor, which was for White patrons only. Black people were only supposed to sit in the balcony, despite the fact that their families had been in the province for over a century by that time. What was the response? She was forcibly removed from the theatre, jailed for a night, and fined (for the one-cent tax on the more expensive seat). She fought the case and lost (Steckley, 2015).

Viola wanted to become a beautician, but no beautician training school in Nova Scotia would admit Black students, so she had to go to Montreal, Atlantic City, and finally New York City to get her training. Once fully qualified, she returned to Halifax to start Vi's Studio of Beauty Culture, also opening the Desmond School of Beauty Culture, the first such school in Nova Scotia (and probably Canada) to cater to Black students.

Her sister, Wanda Robson, published a book about Viola entitled *Sister to Courage: Stories from the World of Viola Desmond, Canada's Rosa Parks*. This was in 2010, the same year that the Nova Scotia government issued her a posthumous pardon. I ended the newsletter article with these words concerning the Robson book: "This is not in our library." It *is* in the Humber library now, along with copies of numerous articles about Viola Desmond and Graham Reynolds and Wanda Robson's 2006 book, *Viola Desmond's Canada: A History of Blacks and Racial Segregation in the Promised Land*.

In 2018, Viola became the first Canadian-born woman to appear alone on a Canadian bank note—a ten-dollar bill. The same year she was honoured by being named a National Historic Person.

In 2020, for the race and ethnicity chapter in the fifth edition of my textbook *Elements of Sociology*, I added a discussion of something that I had no clue about before, the Black Settlement in Alberta, known also as the Black One Thousand (see Appendix A to this chapter). There is so much about Black Canadian history that is not part of general sociological and historical knowledge, even for those Canadian professors like me who taught sociology and related subjects, and who had taken courses on race in the 1970s and 1980s. The Race and Racism course I took in my second or third year as an undergraduate at York University dealt a lot with African Americans, as it was taught by a White American sociologist. I learned nothing in that course about Canadian Black history.

John Steckley

Finding Sophia Bethena Jones

In 2022, I wanted to add the name of the first Black Canadian female doctor to the new edition of my textbook (found now in Steckley, 2023:454–5). I thought that it would be a simple task to accomplish, probably taking an hour or so of research at the most. I was wrong. First one day, then the next I was frustrated in not finding out who such a person was, and how she managed to accomplish what she did. Apparently no one person had been 'officially' assigned that historic honour, certainly no one that I could find. Sources that I expected would inform me told me nothing.

Fortunately, Sonia Hoy, a friend and colleague of mine from Humber who likes to "research things," came across the name Sophia Bethena Jones, who was born in Chatham, in southwestern Ontario, a northern 'station' of the Underground Railroad through which American slaves entered Canada. Sophia B. Jones became a doctor in 1885. I could find no Canadian Black female doctor who graduated at an earlier date. As I researched her life, with the thought of possibly extending mention in the textbook into a scholarly article, I began to learn that there were a good number of members of the Jones family whose achievements were similarly amazing, and whose stories I also thought should be told.

I have a theory concerning why Sophia B. Jones is not well-known. One reason is that her medical education and her many accomplishments all occurred in the U.S., a country that we often contrast ourselves favourably with when it comes to the treatment of Black people. I suspect that her lack of recognition in Canada may have been symptomatic of a kind of patriotic narrowmindedness found sometimes in this country. Whoever wrote her Wikipedia biography summed up the situation with succinct brilliance, when writing in the first sentence that she was "a Canadian-born American medical doctor" (Anonymous, "Sophia B. Jones," Wikipedia). I would add to that that she was Canadian-raised, and would have been inspired by the achievements of the Black people in her town of Chatham, including male doctors (see chapter four). She chose to move to the U.S. as that was where opportunities to be educated in and practice medicine were to be found, opportunities that were not available in Canada at the time.

As noted earlier, at first I planned to write about Sophia B. Jones in an academic article. This plan expanded when I began to learn about the fascinating lives of her paternal great-grandfather, grandfather, and father, her aunts and uncles, and her siblings, primarily her sisters. I could not tell her story completely without including theirs as well. Learning about the British Columbia connection with three of her paternal uncles necessitated a trip to the archives of Salt Spring Island in British Columbia (we had been headed to Vancouver Island to visit an old friend and family members). The very helpful staff there taught me that I had a lot still to learn, a by then familiar lesson that pointed me in the direction of writing this book.

In what I hope is a positive way, this book is something like a textbook (I have written textbooks in sociology, physical anthropology, and Indigenous studies) in that it includes recommended readings and chapter appendices, but also in that the information is presented with the hope of encouraging readers to continue on their path of discovery. It can be revealing and rewarding, as it certainly has been for me, and still continues to be.

I did succeed in writing and publishing a short article in 2023 concerning Sophia Bethena Jones entitled "Canada's First Black Woman to Earn a Medical Degree" for *The Journal of Blacks in Education*. The editor did not know about her before reading my article.

Appendix: The Black One Thousand

In the late nineteenth century, many African-Americans living in the eastern United States moved west to find a place where they felt that they would be free from prejudice and discrimination. In Oklahoma, they established all-black communities, but many of these towns' Black residents, feeling crowded out and decidedly unwelcome, later travelled north in search of a new frontier to settle. A primary event causing this migration took place in 1921, in the relatively successful Black community of Greenwood (known at the time as the Black Wall Street), in which the majority of Tulsa's 10,000-some African-Americans lived. Hundreds of African-Americans were killed, thousands left homeless. Once referred to by the watered-down name of the Tulsa Race Riot, recently it has become more accurately labeled as the Tulsa Race Massacre (see Ellsworth, n.d.).

Western Canada looked like a promising destination for those wanting to escape. Harrison Sneed (see Anonymous, 2010), a Baptist minister from an all-Black town called Clearview, went first to scout the land. The federal government granted him land far north in Alberta, where White settlers did not want to live and farm. And so, in 1909, Sneed returned to Alberta with a group of 194 men, women, and children. They carried more than just their hopes for the future: they brought two hundred rail cars filled with their baggage, livestock, and other possessions. A group of two hundred Black settlers followed shortly after, primarily in 1910 and 1911. A few Black settlements were established in the Albertan countryside. But it was not quite the safe haven from racism they had hoped for.

The White citizens of Edmonton responded predictably in 1911. They issued a petition to the federal government, signed by roughly one-quarter of the city's 24,000 residents. It included the words:

> We, the undersigned residents of the city of Edmonton, respectfully urge upon your attention and upon that of the Government of which you are the head, the serious menace to the future welfare of a large portion of Western Canada, by reason of the alarming influx of negro settlers. ... Last year several hundred negroes arrived in Edmonton and settled in surrounding territory. Already this season nearly three hundred have arrived; and the statement is made ... [that] the advent of such negroes as are now here was most unfortunate for the country, and that further arrivals in large numbers would be disastrous. We cannot admit as any factors the argument that these people may be good farmers or good citizens. It is a matter of common knowledge that it has been proved in the United States that negroes and whites cannot live in proximity without the occurrence of revolting lawlessness and the development of bitter race hatred (from the *Edmonton Capital*, 25 April 1911, as quoted in Cobb, 2017, p. 19).

Canadian Prime Minister Wilfrid Laurier (the man on our five-dollar bill) accepted the petition that year, declaring a prohibition of "any immigrants belonging to the Negro race, which race is deemed unsuitable to the climate and requirements of Canada" (Cobb, 2017, p. 19). By 1914, the immigration that had resulted in the settlement of "The Black One Thousand," as they were known, had ended.

Amber Valley

The main community of the Black Albertans was Amber Valley, which at one point had around 300 citizens. In 1926, they formed a baseball team (see picture in Steckley, 2023:239) that competed with White teams in northern Alberta, and was a popular attraction in the area.

Amber Valley eventually ceased to be an active community, with the small

Amber Valley Museum, Obadiah Place, the small former home of Black pastor Obadiah Bowen, and the old baseball diamond reflecting the past of the community.

Still, some families remained in the province. The first Black Canadian woman to become a lawyer, and the first Black person to be admitted to the Alberta Bar, was a descendant of one of these families, the King family (see chapter four). She was the only woman in her graduating class in Law School—she overcame a double prejudice.

References

Anonymous, 2010, "Sneed and Saunders Familes," *Alberta's Black Pioneer Heritage*, Archive-It. http://wayback.archive-it.org › blackpioneers › people

Bingham, Russell, 2013, "Viola Desmond," *The Canadian Encyclopedia*, January 27, updated by Eli Yarhi, April 16, 2021.

Cobb, Russell, 2017, "Dreams of a Black Oklahoma: On the Trail of the Forgotten Okies of Alberta," *Race-Reader: A Literary Chronicle of Conflict and Oppression in Middle America*, (Tulsa, OK: This Land Press), pp.15–21.

Creese, Gillian, 2020, *"Where Are You From?" Growing Up African-Canadian in Vancouver* (Toronto: University of Toronto Press).

Ellsworth, Scott, n.d., "Tulsa Race Massacre", *The Encyclopedia of Oklahoma History and Culture*.

Howell, Francis Lewis, 1843, *The Toronto Directory and Street Guide for 1843-4* (Toronto: H. A. & W.Rowsell), https://digitalarchive.tpl.ca/objects/243195/the-toronto-directory-and-street-guide-for-1843-4.

Reynolds, Graham, with Wanda Robson, 2016, *Viola Desmond's Canada: A History of Blacks and Racial Segregation in the Promised Land* (Halifax: Fernwood Publishing).

Robson, Wanda, and Donald Caplan, 2010, *Sister to Courage: Stories from the World of Viola Desmond, Canada's Rosa Parks* (Sydney, NS: Breton Books).

Steckley, John, 2015, "Black Canadian history month—eh?," *Newsbreak*, February, page 8.

-----, 2023, "Sophia Bethena Jones: Canada's First Black Woman to Earn a Medical Degree," October 18, *The Journal of Blacks in Higher Education*.

Whitfield, Harvey Amani (Bryan Cummins and John Steckley, eds.), 2004, *From American Slaves to Canadian Citizens: The Case of the Black Refugees 1813–1840* (Toronto: Pearson Canada), Canadian Ethnographic Series.

-----, 2006, *Blacks on the Border: The Black Refugees in British North America, 1815–1860* (Hanover, NH: University of New England).

-----, 2015, *North to Bondage: Loyalist Slaves in the Maritimes* (Vancouver: UBC Press).

-----, 2018, editor, *Black Slaves in the Maritimes: A History in Documents* (Peterborough, ON: Broadview Press).

-----, 2022, *Biographical Dictionary of Enslaved Black People in the Maritimes* (Toronto: University of Toronto Press), Studies in Atlantic Canada.

Wikipedia, n.d., "Viola Desmond."

CHAPTER TWO

Sophia's Great Grandfather, Grandfather and Father

In order to understand Sophia's strength, courage, and determination, it helps a great deal to see what challenges family members before her had to confront. Stories would have been told to her (and successes witnessed) that were likely to develop at least in part the strength of her character.

Great Grandfather Charles Jones

Sophia's paternal great grandfather, Charles Jones, was born in Africa sometime around 1759 and died in the United States around 1841. He was captured, apparently as a child, and then brought by ship to America where he was sold into slavery in North Carolina. The slaver who first bought him was George Jeffrey of Raleigh. Both 'Charles' and 'Jones' were fairly common names given to slaves at the time; 'Charles Jones' was not a name he bore before he was a slave. Unfortunately, we do not know his birth name, the African people and country of his origin, or the year that his ship sailed to America. The name of his wife does not appear to be known today, nor are the names of any of their children (if they had any) other than Allen Jones. In 1830 there would be some 245,601 slaves in the state, roughly one third of the total population of 737,987 of North Carolina at the time (Wikipedia, 2022). It truly was a slave state.

Grandfather Allen Jones (1794–1877)

Allen Jones was born in Raleigh, North Carolina, and grew up on the North Carolina plantation where his father was a slave, a status which he, of course, inherited. But he was ambitious and opportunistic. He developed skills in blacksmithing and gunsmithing. He married a woman named Temperance 'Polly' Josephson Craven.[2] She was born enslaved in 1801, her owner proba-

---

2. Her maiden name is generally presented as 'Josephson' but on her son Elias T. Jones' death certificate it is given as 'Craven'.

bly being John Busbee, who sold her in 1807 as "one negro girl named Tempy" to John Moore, who in turn would sell her to Stephen and Delia Haywood, probably in 1811. She was sold again in 1828 to Charles Parish and Parker Rand. Her next and final purchaser was her husband Allen Jones on January 15, 1829, who also bought his own freedom and that of their three children and his father.[3] He had earned the money with his blacksmithing skills by working for himself when he wasn't working for his 'master'. This included shoeing horses on Sundays. There isn't complete agreement in the literature as to how much he paid for the freedom of his family. There is a story suggesting that he was first told he would have to be pay $2,000, which took him some time to accumulate, then the price went up either another $1,000 to $3,000, or another $3,000 to total $5,000, either way a king's ransom. One possible reason for this increase apart from slave owner greed was as time passed, his sons grew older and stronger and therefore better able to do hard work in the fields, hence raising their value to their slave owner. His father's price, it is said, was only $350, but then he was a relatively old man of seventy, whose capacity to work in the fields or do other hard physical labour value would probably not have been very great.

One extensive account of Allen Jones' purchasing his freedom and that of his family is found in the writings of C. S. Hopkins. He was a resident of Oberlin, a town the significance of which for the education of the Jones family will be stressed shortly. Hopkins was just a boy when the Jones family arrived there. He received much of his information from Allen's son, Elias T. Jones. Note that the figures quoted are different from those of other reports:

> While he was a slave in Raleigh, N.C., he bought his freedom by shoeing horses on Sundays. Fifteen hundred dollars was the price. When he paid the last dollar his master went back on him and said: 'You are my nigger yet, and I have the money too.' Jones didn't give up, but started the second time to obtain his freedom and by the help of some friends he was enabled to bet his papers by paying thirteen hundred dollars more. He afterwards purchased his wife and three of his children,[4] and also accumulated considerable property (Hopkins, 1845).

---

3. There are no references to his purchasing his mother's freedom, so I am assuming that she had died before this time.
4. The other four to be mentioned later were not yet born.

Allen Jones very much desired to move his family from the slave state of North Carolina to a free state. He had several very good reasons for wanting to do that. He had built a school for Black students that had been burned down three times by those opposing education for African Americans. It is unlikely that any charges were ever laid on the white arsonists involved. An additional incentive for Allen to leave was that in 1839 the Constitution of North Carolina was amended to take away the right of freed slaves to vote.

In October 1842, although a freed slave, Allen Jones was dragged from his home and was "shockingly whipped" (Franklin 1995:92). He had earlier appeared before the Anti-Slavery Convention in New York, presenting a speech on the subject of his being 'tarred and feathered' in Raleigh (Franklin 1995:125). This was likely the main trigger for the whipping.

The editor of the *Raleigh Register* wrote of the whipping in a way that condemned both the racist offenders and their victim. He referred to Allen Jones as "[h]aving imprudently returned to Raleigh" after presenting his speech. The editor goes on to say:

> We hope that the good people of Raleigh will not stop short of the most condign[5] punishment of this outrage, not because of the individual against whom it was perpetrated (for *we suspect that he is deserving of no sympathy*), but for the sake of LAW, which we desire to be upheld against all infractions (Raleigh *Register*, October 1842, as quoted in Franklin 1995:92; emphasis added).

In another very similar newspaper account entitled "Disgraceful Outrage," the writer, while arguing against the immorality of taking the law into one's own hands, loses no opportunity to speak ill of the victim as well:

> A free man of colour, named ALLEN JONES, a Blacksmith by trade, *who has rendered himself obnoxious*, was forcibly taken from his own house, in the dead of night, by a mob, and so beaten, bruised and mangled, that doubts are entertained of his recovery. Now with regard to *Allen Jones, he may be a bad man, and, for argument's sake, we will admit that he is a great rascal,* but that fact affords no plea of justification or excuse in the world, for the outrage which has been perpetrated (Franklin 1995:92; emphasis added).

5. This word 'condign' means 'deserved, appropriate'.

On December 6, 1842, the following advertisement for Allen Jones' property was published in the *Raleigh Register*, placed by Seth Jones,[6] Parker Rand, and D. W. Stone. It would appear that Allen Jones had been prosperous enough in his trade to be able to purchase a significant amount of property:

> Sale of Valuable Property In and near the City of Raleigh
> The Subscribers will offer for sale at Public Vendue on Saturday, the 24th day of December next the following property belonging to Allen Jones (Blacksmith,) vis: House and Lot part of Lot No. 128 … 140 feet and running back 91 feet on which is a good two story wood Dwelling House and the necessary out houses.
>
> The Blacksmith shop, part of the same Lot No. 128, at the corner of Hargett and Blount streets, fronting 91 feet on Hargett, and 75 feet on Blount street, on which there is a good Blacksmith's shop and coal shed, a small Dwelling House and Stable.
>
> And in the Southeastern suburbs of the City, a few hundred yards beyond the Corporation limits, … the Lot on which the said Allen Jones now lives, containing about two acres, on which there is a good two story Dwelling House and the necessary out houses, with a well of excellent water in the yard.
>
> And two acres of land adjoining the Dwelling House, and fronting on the road, on which there are two small houses with two rooms each
>
> And about an acre and a half of ground, fronting the Dwelling House Lot, and on the opposite side of the road. This will be divided into half acre lots and are good building sites, all of which will be sold on the premises.
>
> There will also be sold on the same day at the Blacksmith shop two full sets of Blacksmith's tools, two Anvils and two Smith's Bellowses. …
>
> The title to all of the above property is believed to be unquestionable. (Jones, Rand and Stone 1842)

In March 1843, Allen Jones took his family in a covered wagon from North Carolina to Ohio, which, unlike North Carolina, was a free state. They were accompanied by two other families.

They went to Oberlin, situated in northern Ohio, a little southwest of

---

6. To the best of my knowledge, he was not related to the Jones family discussed here. As mentioned earlier, Jones was a common name given to slaves.

Cleveland, where there was a college which admitted Black students (see discussion below).

In an advertisement entitled "Stop the Runaway," placed in the Raleigh paper of March 7, we see that Allen may have assisted in the freedom of another slave. That is certainly what the writer of the ad was claiming. After describing in great detail his nineteen-year-old runaway slave, named Calvin Terry, slave owner Joseph B. Hinton wrote the following, condemning Allen Jones for stealing his human property:

> He was doubtless lured off, to drive their wagon to Cincinnati, Ohio by the family of free negroes, (the family of Allen Jones of *lynching* notoriety,) which left here the night before. If Calvin has free papers, they are forged, and most probably by said Allen Jones himself, who has been the subject of *indictment* in our Superior Court for an offence of that kind (Hinton, 1843).

I have found no evidence that Calvin Terry was ever returned to his former owner. It is highly unlikely that he ever was. The Jones family had successfully rescued him.

The above quoted C. S. Hopkins wrote about his positive first impressions of Allen Jones in his early years in Oberlin:

> The writer remembers when they arrived in town. They came in on South Main street with their covered wagon. He soon had a shop built.... There he worked, early and late, pounding out the dollars to pay for educating his children. He always seems happy and cheerful; he used to sing a great deal while at work.... He would sing and keep time with his hammer on the anvil. When a boy, I well remember hearing him in the early morning air. It used to sound very musical (Hopkins, 1845).

Allen Jones clearly wanted his children to learn a trade. Four of his sons graduated from Oberlin College in northern Ohio. Oberlin College was founded in 1833 by a Presbyterian minister and missionary who had strong anti-slavery, abolitionist views, providing a stop along the Underground Railroad. In 1835 it became the first American college to admit Black students. In 1841, it became the first college in the U.S. to offer a Bachelor of Arts to women in a co-educational program.

Oberlin and Oberlin College

The educational institution and town of Oberlin played an important role in the stories of the Jones family as told in this work. The defining qualities of the community were born out of fairly radical religious ideas of equality, which were opposed to both the racism and the sexism of the time. The name 'Oberlin' honoured John Frederick Oberlin, a German pastor whose life was dedicated to the poor in Alsace, in eastern France. The man was involved in establishing schools, building roads, and introducing the learning of the trades of masonry and blacksmithing to people who were poor.

The founders, the Reverend John Jay Shipherd (1802–1844) and Philo Penfield Stewart (1798–1868), shared a dream or religious vision of establishing both a school and a religious colony simultaneously. The result was a success, particularly in terms of developing a school that benefited Blacks and women who wanted to receive a good education that they could not get otherwise. The following is a timeline of some of the early achievements of the school.

1833: Began as Oberlin Collegiate Institute[7] (with twenty-nine male and fifteen female students).
1835: Admitted Black male students (first predominantly White school to do so).
1838: Admitted female students in diploma courses (called the 'Ladies Course').
1841: Offered male/female co-educational courses for B.A., another first.
1844: Educated George Boyer Vashon (later to be an attorney, scholar, professor, essayist, and poet). He was the First Black student there to earn a B.A. (enrolled in 1840 at sixteen years old). See the Appendix for more information about this man and his accomplishments.
1862: Mary Jane Patterson received a B.A. in Education, the first African American woman to earn a degree at an American college.[8]

Oberlin College and Black Students

On December 15, 1834, Shipherd wrote a letter to the Board of Trustees of Oberlin College, asking that they pass his non-negotiable resolution in favour of having black students:

---

[7]. This does not mean that the founders had intended it to be just a high school. They did not. The name would eventually be changed to Oberlin College.
[8]. See https://www2.oberlin.edu/external/EOG/OYTT-images/MJPatterson.html

'*Resolved*, that students shall be received into this Institution *irrespective of color*.' This should be passed because it is a right principle, and God will bless us in doing right. Also because thus doing right we gain the confidence of benevolent and able men, who probably will furnish us some thousands.... Indeed, if our Board would violate right so as to reject youth of talent and piety because they were *black*, I should have *no heart* to labor for the upbuilding of our Seminary, believing that the curse of God would come upon us (Fairchild 1883:53).

Some of the other members of the board were concerned about the potential negative effects of letting in Black students; that it might, for example, cause the parents of White students to take their children out of the school, or not send them there to begin with, maybe even leave the town. However the principal colonists of the Oberlin community supported Shipherd's proposal. The Board of Trustees eventually narrowly voted in favour of the school admitting Black students in 1835. It was so close that the president of the Board had to break a tie in the voting.

In writing about the history of Oberlin college up until 1883, James Harris Fairchild,[9] the president of the college at that time, estimated the number of Black students that the college had, and wrote about the principles of equality that supported having them at the school:

From 1840 to 1860 the proportion of colored students was four or five per cent. Soon after the [Civil] war the ratio rose to seven or eight per cent but has fallen again to five or six in a hundred. No adaptation of the course of study to the special needs of colored pupils was ever made. It was not a colored school that was proposed, but a school where colored students should have equal privileges with others. No record of colored students has been kept distinct from the general record. No distinctive mark appears in the catalogues. The only reliance for the past is the knowledge and memory of instructors and others.

Among the 20,000 different pupils that have been in attendance from the beginning probably 1000 have been colored. Sixty have completed a course—thirty-two young men and twenty-eight young

---

9. Fairchild had been a freshman at the college in 1834, graduated in 1838, then went from being a tutor to a professor of Latin and Greek. He was the third president of the college, serving from 1866 to 1889, and after resigning from the position serving again in 1896–8 as acting president.

women. Some of these were brilliant scholars, some have attained to distinction, and most are occupying positions of usefulness in the land (Fairchild, 1883:111–2).

Fairchild also commented on what he believed brought Black families to the town of Oberlin:

> The same action which brought colored students to the school, brought colored families to the town to find their homes. At first, some of the more prosperous of the free colored people of the Slave States came in to secure privileges for themselves and their children. Some of the more enterprising of the slaves at length heard of Oberlin, and crept in stealthily to see whether what they had heard was true. Some of these found courage to remain and thus the colored element gradually increased until it has become a fifth part of the population (Fairchild 1883:113–4).

The Jones family was one such example, as he would note when presenting the names without distinction of race, of "the families that came early and remained until the later years." (Fairchild 1883:296). They definitely benefited from what town and college offered them.

It wasn't a completely racially idyllic life in Oberlin. C. S. Hopkins wrote about a fight between White and Black boys at the school, which involved both John Craven Jones and William Allen Jones. The teacher blamed the White boys, and punished them accordingly (Hopkins, 1845).

The Jones Family and Oberlin College

Name	Graduating Year
Charles Brougham Jones	1847–49 (non-graduate)
James B. Jones	1840s?; reached junior year
James Monroe Jones	1849
John Craven Jones	1856
William Allen Jones	1857
Elias Toussaint Jones	1859
Bethany Jones	Did not complete degree
Blanche Virginia Harris Jones (Elias T.'s wife)	1860

| Almira Scott Jones (John Craven' wife) | 1870 |
| Anna Holland Jones | 1875 |

Oberlin College Numbers

In 1866, J. H. Fairchild, in his inaugural speech as president of Oberlin College, declared:

> As the immediate numerical result, our catalogue presents the names of 243 who have taken the Theological course, 502 who have graduated from College, and 392 who have completed the Ladies' course of four years, in all 1,137 graduates; and some fifteen thousand others who have enjoyed the advantages of the school for a single year or more. (Fairchild, 1866)

James Monroe Jones, Sophia's Father

Sophia's father was named James Monroe Jones (1821–1906). He would have been given that name as a mark of respect for James Monroe (1758–1831), the fifth American president who served during the years 1817–1825. Although President James Monroe was a slave owner, he signed the Missouri Compromise which, among other features, enabled some states to be 'free states' (see discussion in the next chapter of the implications of the overriding of that law), and was a supporter of the American Colonization Society, which promoted the return of American slaves to Africa in the now independent country known as Liberia (the name based on the word 'liberty').

James Monroe Jones earned a Bachelor of Science degree at Oberlin College, graduating in 1849. He was only the fourth African American to do so. It appears that he may have had a relatively well-rounded education there. In the commentary included in a piece about a rifle he made that is kept in the Windsor Museum, the unnamed writer mentions another ability he had, a flair for languages: "He is said to have been able to speak seven languages, including Latin." This might be only a slight exaggeration, except for the Latin. James Harris Fairchild, then president of Oberlin College, wrote in 1883 of five languages that were a significant feature in what was taught there: "The study of the ancient languages, Latin, Greek and Hebrew, has always held a prominent place, and linguistic study is quite as prominent to-day as at any time in the past.…The modern languages, French and German, have claimed their share of attention" (Fairchild, 1883:256).

James Monroe knew Latin well enough that local schoolchildren in Chatham would go to his workshop after school for assistance with the language.

A copy exists of an undated article written by a D. Arnold, entitled "Assignment: Bringing J. M. Jones Back from the Grave." Reflecting the typical obscurity in which Jones family member accomplishments exist, Arnold wrote: "This story starts in 1951, when the Ohio State University first heard about Jones from a man in Ontario who said he [Jones] was the 1st black man to graduate from that institution of higher learning" (Arnold, n.d.).

Like his father, and probably learning a lot from him, James Monroe Jones became a gunsmith. He moved north to Chatham in southwest Ontario, then known as Upper Canada, in 1852. He became well known under the nickname 'Gunsmith Jones', and he had a shop in town for selling the products of his work.

His gunsmithing ability was very much appreciated at the time. In the words of well-travelled Samuel Ringold Ward, in his published autobiography of 1855, "James Madison[10] Jones of Chatham, has not the superior as a gunsmith in Canada, if indeed in North America" (Ward, 1855).

In a delightfully worded article written by Gary Simser, entitled "The Prince & the Pistols: James 'Gunsmith' Jones' gift was fit for royalty, his patrimony was not," James' handiwork became a subject of some racist distress among some of the leading figures of Chatham regarding a visit in September 1860 by Edward, the Prince of Wales (1841–1910). Then still a teenager, the eldest son of Queen Victoria and Prince Albert would later become King Edward VII. He was the first member of British royalty to visit Canada while not on military service:[11]

> The prince had been persuaded to divert his first extensive official Canadian tour to Chatham, Ontario, in order to accept a finely crafted pair of derringer pistols made by a local gunsmith and engraver of coffin-plates and Canadian Pacific Railway dining-car silverware.... the prince arrived promptly in his royal coach at the Chatham rail station where he unexpectedly found himself twiddling his thumbs for ten minutes while local officials earnestly huddled to solve a last-minute difficulty.... Apparently, a certain prominent citizen named Mr.

---

10. He is mistaken here in James Monroe Jones' middle name.
11. In 1786–7, the future King William IV came to Canada as part of a naval contingent. In 1791–1800, Prince Edward, father of Queen Victoria, came to Canada as part of his military duties.

McKellar had been informed, much too late, that a Black businessman and manufacturer named James Monroe "Gunsmith" Jones had made the gift of derringer pistols.

Confronted with a dilemma, the local pooh-bahs had precious little time to smooth it over. One can only imagine the tension of red-faced locals … as they strained to find a way out of their predicament….

Oh, to have been a fly on the wall, to have seen the tight-throated demeanour of whoever was selected to duly inform an impatient prince that there had been, ahem, a change in plans; that the derringers had been made by *contaminated hands* and as such could not be presented to a member of the Royal Family (Simser, 2018, emphasis added).

You could imagine, as well, the extreme disappointment that James and his family felt about the whole affair.

James married Emily T. Francis (1829–1914), a native of Elizabeth City, New Jersey, on November 16, 1854, in London, not too far away. They had six children, four girls and two boys. Sophia was their second child.

It is unfortunate I could not find out anything about Emily other than her name, the American city and state in which she was born, and the fact that one child was named after her. Since I could find nothing about her going to Oberlin, and because she bore six children, it is most likely that she did not become a teacher.

Gunsmith Jones was especially gifted in making the small or 'pocket' pistols known as derringers. He won awards for his work crafting these guns. In 1859, he won a medal for his derringer entry at the California State Agricultural Society. Later he won first prize at the Montreal Manufacturing and Trade Fair, at the Grand Provincial Exhibition opened by the previously mentioned avid gun collector the Prince of Wales, whose title is on the medal that Jones had won. Having seen Gunsmith Jones' excellent handiwork, it should come as no surprise that he took a side trip to Chatham to obtain as a gift three "Newfoundland Dog" engraved derringers.

Apparently, Jones taught one of his daughters to be a silver engraver (Secord, 1960:40). His sister Bethany Jones was recorded as learning that trade as well, although she did become a teacher. In James Secord's remembrance, he says the following about the father and daughter:

James had a daughter whom he taught the art of engraving. They engraved a great deal of C.P.R dining car silverware. He and his daughter engraved a sterling silver platter which was presented to Queen Victoria on a ceremonial oc[c]asion" (Secord, 1960).

Concerning that platter, the following letter of inquiry was sent to Sir Michael Adeane, the private secretary to Queen Elizabeth, on January 7, 1961. It was sent by the curator of a Canadian Pacific Railway Museum. It reads as follows:

Information has come to my attention that one James M. Jones, of Chatham, Ontario, with the assistance of his daughter, once engraved a silver platter which was presented to Queen Victoria on a ceremonial occasion.

If it is possible to determine anything from such fragmentary information I should be most interested to know if this platter still exists.

Unfortunately, I know nothing of either the date or the occasion of presentation. The only additional pertinent information at my disposal is that Jones engraved a great deal of Canadian Pacific Railway dining car silverware, which might suggest a CPR presentation of the Jones platter to her majesty, perhaps on the occasion of the railway's completion in 1885.

This museum is interested in developing a significant collection of Canadian firearms, and it happens that Jones is chiefly remembered as being the finest gunsmith that Canada ever produced, as well as this country's first Negro gunsmith. He produced firearms between 1857 and 1892. Examples of Jones' craftsmanship are eagerly sought after by collectors all over North America, and we count ourselves fortunate in having three Jones guns, including the over-and-under combination piece that may well be unique in Canadian production. Thus anything relating to Jones is of the highest possible interest to us (1961).

I don't know whether the curator received a reply, but I have received no substantial evidence from employees of the museum to support the assumption that one of Jones-made silver platters was given to Queen Victoria. James Monroe and his daughter are said to have engraved silver platters for the dining cars of the Canadian Pacific Railway, and there are several railway museums in Canada that could have such platters, of which I would very much like to see pictures. No luck so far has come from my e-mails to such museums. I suspect that the sheer size of their collections might be one good reason for that.

Another source (Randal in Smith, 2018) claimed that the gifts to Queen Victoria also included derringers made by Gunsmith Jones, although I have not yet been able to verify that claim either.

I did receive (August 21, 2023) an e-mail from Simon Metcalf, the King's Armourer, who works at the appropriate museum, and he stated that he could not find any evidence of such a gift being found in the museum.

John Brown's Rifle

John Brown was a White American man who wanted to abolish the slave trade. And if it took overthrowing the American government to do that, he was willing to give that a try. In late April 1858 he went to Chatham, which he knew to be a community that was involved with the Underground Railroad and was populated with many Black people, including those that were relatively well-to-do and influential. That would, of course, include James Monroe Jones.

In 1850, the Fugitive Slave Act had been passed, making for a dangerous situation for escaped slaves living in the 'free' states, and leading to an increase in the number of Black people coming to Chatham, and to Canada generally, an estimated 15,000 to 20,000 between 1850 to 1860.

Brown needed volunteer soldiers and money. James had been able to help him with the latter, sources conflicting over whether that was in 1850 or 1858 or both. In a deal that appears to be either a pawning or a loan, John Brown left his rifle with James, in return for which James would give him $75, quite a bit of money at the time—equivalent to $2,300 in today's currency, according to one writer (Levitin, 2017). The gun may have been some form of assurance that Brown would return and pay back the loan.

Brown's rifle can be seen today in the Chatham-Kent Black Historical Society and Black Mecca Museum, located on King Street in Chatham, the street upon which the Jones family lived. There are also two of the rifles that Jones himself made. The museum is contained in only one room, part of a larger municipal complex, but a visit there provides significant insight into Black history in Chatham, including several pictures and stories relating to the Jones family.

On May 8 and 10, a Constitution Convention was held in a local Baptist church in Chatham, with thirty-four Black people and twelve whites attending. The former included leading abolitionist and Underground Railroad leader Harriet Tubman (c.1820–1913), with whom James would be quite familiar as she had visited Chatham on more than one occasion. Her significance at the time is summarized in the following excerpt from a short but perceptive biography:

> Known as the 'Moses of her people,' Harriet Tubman was enslaved, escaped, and helped others gain their freedom as a 'conductor' of the Underground Railroad. Tubman also served as a scout, spy, guerrilla soldier and nurse for the Union Army during the Civil War. She is considered the first African American woman to serve in the military…. Her success led slave owners to post a $40,000 reward for her capture or death (Michals, 2015).

At the convention, a planned action against the U.S. federal government was discussed, among other radical steps. James signed the declaration, but decided not to leave Chatham for Brown's planned attack on Harper's Ferry, West Virginia, where there was a government arsenal that supplied the American army with guns. Every other Black Chatham member of the delegation made the same decision, except for one (see below). It would probably and rightfully have seemed too dangerous and impractical to them.

John Brown left for Kansas in June. On October 16, 1859, twenty-two men, including five Black men, headed for Harper's Ferry. They would be defeated, and Brown was tried and hanged for treason. As stated earlier, the gun remained with James, and subsequently his descendants.

One member of the Chatham Black community, Osbourne Perry Anderson (1830–1872), who was born in Pennsylvania and joined the community in 1850, went with Brown to Harper's Ferry. He was one of only five (and the only Black man) to survive the experience. In 1861, he self-published an account of John Brown's work in a short book entitled *A Voice from Harper's Ferry: A Narrative of Events at Harper's Ferry; with Incidents Prior and Subsequent to its Capture by Captain Brown and His Men.*[12]

James Monroe also wrote an account of the life of John Brown in 1883,

---

12. https://www.historyisaweapon.com/defcon1/andersonvoiceharpersferry.html#:~:text=Seventeen%20whites%20and%20five%20blacks,1%20narrative%20of%20the%20raid

published in Cleveland (Arnold, n.d.). In 1874, he would receive the great honour of being appointed as the Chatham Justice of the Peace, an honour typically given in nineteenth-century Canada to successful tradesmen, merchants, and farmers. In response to an 1875 Oberlin College survey of graduate occupations, he wrote, doubtless with well-earned pride: "Justice of the Peace, appointed for life. By the Government and Governor-General." He was the first Black man to have that honour in Canada.

In a short piece written by a Mrs. Huff, who spoke with three individuals who had known Gunsmith Jones when they were young, one of them, Archie Thibeault, who lived in Jones' house in 1907, informed her that: "His clearest memory is of the sign which Jones had in front of his house—a large wooden gun-shaped sign which attracted the eyes of the boys. His shop was a front room of the house" (Huff, n.d.).

Jones retired from the gun trade at age 71, moving to Ann Arbour, Michigan to live with his son George A. M. Jones, who was the only child of his still living in the area. James Monroe died at 85 in 1906.

His gunsmithing is still looked upon with great respect. According to one modern commentator:

His derringers are extreme[ly] rare, and proudly collected by avid private gun collectors. Although several of his accuracy renowned gun barrels can be found on rifles made by other less gifted gunsmiths, there remain only a very few complete (denoted by both his attentive quality style, and JMJ engraved lock) JMJ rifles in existence (Smith, 2018; "Randal" commenting).

In November 2014, "A very rare silver-and-gold mounted Philadelphia-style Percussion Derringer" sold in auction for $6,435 American, approximately $8,252 Canadian.

In the Chatham-Kent Black Mecca Museum and the Windsor Museum, there are a number of examples of his gun-making craft (http://windsormuseum.ca:8080/mwebcgi/mweb.exe?request=record;id=31594;type=101).

Appendix: George Boyer Vashon's Timeline of Achievement

1844: Graduated from Oberlin College.
1847: Rejected from practicing law in Pennsylvania.
1848: Passed the bar in New York (the first AfricanAmerican to do so).

1849: Professor of Languages in Haiti.

1850: Returned to New York to become the state's first Black lawyer; would eventually become a Supreme Court lawyer.

1854–7: Professor.

1867–8: Co-founder and professor at Howard University.

2010: Admitted to the bar in Pennsylvania posthumously.

2015: Establishment of George B. Vachon Museum of African American History in St. Louis.

References

Ancestry.ca (under "James Monroe Jones" as living until 1856 https://www.ancestry.ca/genealogy/records/james-monroe-jones-24-7yf97r

Anonymous, n.d., "Allen Jones (1794–1877), WikiTree.

Anonymous, n.d., "Temperance (Unknown Allen)," WikiTree. https://www.wikitree.com/wiki/Unknown-595574

Arnold, D., n.d., "Assignment: Bring J. M. Jones Back from the Grave."

Barker, Gordon S., 2016, "The 'Colored Hero' of Harper's Ferry: John Anthony Copeland and the War Against Slavery, *Civil War Book Review*, vol. 18, no. 2. DOI: 10.31390/cwbr.18.2.07 Available at: https://digitalcommons.lsu.edu/cwbr/vol18/iss2/6

DeMarinis, Jan, Jean Ebosh, and Gail Wood, eds., 1996, *Oberlin: Yesterday, Today, Tomorrow*, 3rd ed., chapter 3. www2.oberlin.edu/external/EOG/OYTT/ch3.html

Fairchild, James Harris, 1866, *Educational Arrangement and College Life, Inaugural Address of President J. H. Fairchild, delivered at The Commencement of Oberlin College*, August 22, Edward O. Jenkins.

-----, 1883, *Oberlin: The Colony and the College, 1833–1883*, E. J. Goodrich, reprinted by BiblioBazaar, 2010.

Five Colleges of Ohio: Denison, Kenyon, Oberlin, Ohio Wesleyan and Woosk, original obituary 1897, "Elias T. Jones Dies at his Home Sunday," http://dcollections.oberlin.edu/digital/collection/p15963coll8/id/114

Franklin, John Hope, 1995 (first edition in 1943), *The Free Negro in North Carolina, 1790–1860*, The University of North Carolina Press, https://archive.org/freenegroinnorthfran_0)djvu

Gilbert, Jim and Lisa, 2022, " 'Gunsmith' Jones an the prince's pistols," *Chatham Daily News*, June 3.

Gooding, S. James, 1970, "James M. Jones of Chatham 'Gunsmith & Maker of fine Derringer Pistols,' " *The Canadian Journal of Arms Collecting*, vol. 8, no. 3.

Hinton, Joseph, B., 1843, "Stop the Runaway," *The Raleigh Register*, March 7, page 3. Newspapers.com (https://www.newspapers.com/clip/104563848/)

Hopkins, C. S., 1845, "Some By-Gone Days: Recollections of an Early Oberlin School, its Teacher and its scholars." *Oberlin News*, Dr.%20Sophia%20B%20Jones/1222-JONES-page210-233%20-%20gun.pdf.

Jones, Seth, Parker Rand and D. W. Stone, "Sale of Valuable Property, In and near the City of Raleigh," *The Raleigh Register*, page 4. https://www.newspapers.com/article/104563295/

Lawson, Ellen N., and Marlene Merrill, 1983, "The antebellum 'Talented Thousandth': Black College Students at Oberlin Before Civil War," *The Journal of Negro Education*, vol. 52, no. 2 (Spring), pp. 142–155.

Lee, Brian, 2023, "A Trailblazer All His Life—New York's First Black Attorney, Admitted 175 Years Ago, Fought for Freedom All the Way to the U.S. Supreme Court." *New York Law Journal*, February 23.

Levitin, Aaron, 2017, "Antislavery in Small Things Research Outcome: The Gun of John Brown," *Antislavery Connections*.

Michals, Debra, 2015, "Harriet Tubman (c.1820–1913)," *National Women's History Museum*, https://www.womenshistory.org/education-resources/biographies/harriet-tubman

Oberlin College and Conservatory, n.d., "Oberlin History," Oberlin.edu/about-oberlin/oberlin-history

Paton-Evans, Karen, 2021, "Gunsmith James Jones: Canada's first Black gunsmith, his part in the Underground Railroad, and his rifle," *The Miller Times* (Miller and Miller Auction Ltd.).

Secord, James, 1960, "Biography of J. M Jones," Dr.%20Sophia%20B%20Jones/1222-JONES-page139-142%20-%20James%20Monroe.pdf'

Simser, Guy, 2018, "The Prince & the Pistols: James 'Gunsmith' Jones' gift was fit for royalty, his patrimony was not", *Canada's History*, February 6. (originally published in the February-March issue of *The Beaver*).

Sjuberg, Gail, 2005, "Salt Spring's first teacher reveals black history lineage," *Gulf Island Driftwood*, February 23 (Salt Spring Island Archives).

Smith, Philip, 2018, "One of the Best Old World Gunsmiths, You've Never Heard Of," *Ammoland—Shooting Sports News*, December 13.

Ward, Samuel Ringold Ward, 1855, *Autobiography of a Fugitive Negro: His Anti-slaving Labours in the United States, Canada & England*, (London: John Snow).

Wikipedia, accessed in 2022, "History of slavery in North Carolina."

Windsor Museum, files pages 143–49.

CHAPTER THREE

Sophia's Uncles and an Aunt

Sophia's uncles and her aunt set examples for her to follow in overcoming the obstacles faced by a Black person in both the United States and Canada. In this chapter, I first discuss three of her uncles, her father's brothers, who followed the gold rush, escaped the tensions of the pre-Civil War years in the U.S., and made their way to the golden possibilities of British Columbia, first when it was a British colony and then as a Canadian province.

Three Jones Brothers and the Black Exodus to British Columbia

During the period 1848 to 1855, there was a gold rush in California that drew a great number of people from many places and backgrounds. It has been calculated that around four thousand African Americans travelled there during this time (Rawls and Orsi, 1999:5). They had an extra incentive besides the gold. Those coming from the slave states of the American South initially believed that they could also gain their freedom there, although that belief proved not to be on solid ground. When the rewards of the California Gold Rush began to dwindle, there was a need to go somewhere else to 'get rich quick', and to achieve freedom. For many African Americans, that somewhere would be British Columbia.

Three Legal Decisions that Contributed to the Black Exodus to British Columbia

But it was not just gold that led African Americans to British Columbia. Three political/legal decisions provided ample reason for African Americans living in California to want to leave the United States. One was the *Dred Scott v. John F. A. Sandford*[13] case. Dred Scott was a slave whose owner took him from the slave state of Missouri to the 'free state' of Wisconsin, where slavery was not legal. When he was brought back to Missouri, he sued for his

---

13. John F. A. Sandford was an extremely wealthy and influential man. His brother-in-law was Scott's 'owner'.

freedom, claiming his time in Wisconsin had made him a free man. The case ended up in the U.S. Supreme Court. Scott lost his case in March 1857, with a 7 to 2 vote, legally cancelling his free status. The Chief Justice declared that African Americans "are not included, and were not intended to be included, under the word 'citizens' in the Constitution, and can therefore claim none of the rights and privileges which that instrument provides for and secures to citizens of the United States" (National Archives).

This decision overturned the Missouri Compromise of 1820, which, among other important changes, had made free states out of all western territories in the U.S. north of Missiouri's southern border. The decision in this case was one of the leading causes of the Civil War.

A similar socially crippling race-based decision was a bill passed in March 1858, the California Assembly's Bill 339. The name of the bill was "An Act to Restrict and Prevent the Immigration of Negroes and Mulattoes." It meant that all Black people in California had to be registered, and many could be captured and taken from the state without any legal protection.

That same month, the back-and-forth case of young Archy Lee (1840–1873) was finally resolved.[14] In the fall of 1857, his slaveowner brought this teenaged slave from Mississippi to California. When Archy learned that his owner was going to take him back to Mississippi, he escaped, but was captured again. The situation was taken to court. In Lee's first court case the judge ruled in his favour, awarding him his freedom. Unsurprisingly, the California Supreme Court overturned this decision and Archy was arrested. In March, 1858, a federal judge overturned that decision. Later that year Archy Lee, eighteen years old, joined the Black exodus to British Columbia. He died a young but free man there in 1873.

In 1858, a delegation representing San Francisco's Black community met with Governor James Douglas in Victoria, who encouraged them to move to the then British colony of Vancouver Island. Their response to this encouragement included the following words:

> We are fully convinced that the continued aim of the spirit and policy of our mother country is to oppress, degrade and entrap us. We have therefore determined to seek continued asylum in the land of strangers

---

14. An informative book on Archy Lee and the situation in California during his days there is Brian McGinty's *Struggle for Freedom: The True Story of California Gold, the Nation's Tragic March Toward Civil War, and a Young Black Man's Fight for Liberty* (Lyon's Press).

from the oppression, prejudice, and relentless persecution that have pursued us from more than two centuries in this our mother country (Cooper, 2018:1093–4).

In short order a number of Black people, estimated at between four hundred and eight hundred, moved to the colony of British Columbia. The positive reports sent back to their people in California encouraged some five hundred more to soon make the move.

The movement of the people known as the 'Black Pioneers' into British Columbia was designated as a National Historic Event by the Government of Canada on September 22, 1997. The text of the plaque unveiled on February 20, 2000, that marked this designation begins with the following words:

In 1858 nearly 800 free Blacks left the oppressive racial conditions of San Francisco for a new life on Vancouver Island. Governor James Douglas had invited them here as promising settlers. Though still faced with intense discrimination, these pioneers enriched the political, religious and economic life of the colony.

In 1859, three of Sophia's uncles, William Allen Jones, John Craven Jones, and Elias Toussaint Jones joined the ranks of the Black Pioneers.

Three Important Leaders of the Black Exodus to British Columbia

The stories of these three men can provide useful information to help understand the nature of the black exodus to British Columbia, and why Sophia's three uncles went there.

Wellington Delaney Moses

Black people wanting to escape California formed a Pioneer Committee, the purpose of which was to investigate the possibility of a move to Victoria on Vancouver Island. A leader of this organization was Wellington Delaney Moses,[15] an African American man born in the West Indies, who had spent most of his adult life to that point as a mariner. His surname of Moses was certainly apt, as he strongly advocated that his people move to Victoria. In a letter to a fellow member of the Pioneer Committee he wrote the following:

---

15. To learn more about Wellington Delaney Moses, read Bill Gallher's historical novel, *A Man Called Moses: The Curious Life of Wellington Delaney Moses* (Touchwood Editions, 2011).

To describe the beauty of the country my pen cannot do it. It is one of the most beautifully level towns I was ever in.... I consider Victoria to be one of the garden spots of this world.... The climate is most beautiful; the strawberry vines and peach trees are in full blow.... All the colored man wants here is ability and money.... *It is a God-sent land for the colored people* (Kilian, 2020a:32; emphasis mine).

He would establish himself as a barber in Victoria, continuing that profession when he moved with other gold miners to mainland British Columbia. He became known as the Black Barber of Barkerville.

Mifflin Wistar Gibbs (1823–1915)[16]

Also worth discussing here is one of the leading figures of the first group of Black immigrants to come to Victoria: Mifflin Wistar Gibbs. Along with Peter Lester he owned the Pioneer Boot and Shoe Emporium in San Francisco. A racist incident took place at that shop that prompted the two men to leave the state and the country for Canada: they could not press charges against two white men who had stolen a pair of shoes from the store and assaulted Lester with a cane.

Gibbs well described the attraction of greater freedom and personal safety he and others like him would acquire in moving out of California to the new colony (as of 1858) of British Columbia:

> [T]here was ever present that spectre of oath [of full citizenship] denial and disenfranchisement, the disheartening consciousness that while our existence was tolerated, we were powerless to appeal to law for the protection of life and property when assailed. British Columbia offered and gave protection to both, and equality of political privileges. I cannot describe with what joy we hailed the opportunity to enjoy that liberty under the "British lion" denied us beneath the pinions of the American Eagle (Gibbs 1902, as quoted in Kahn, 1998:59).

Gibbs met with significant success. With his partner Lester, he ran a store competing with the Hudson's Bay Company. An ad in the *Victoria Gazette* read:

---

16. To learn more about Mifflin Wistar Gibbs, read Crawford Kilian's *Go Do Some Great Thing: The Black Pioneers of British Columbia* (Harbour Publishing, 2020). More information can be gained from Gibbs' autobiography, *Shadow and Light: An Autobiography* (1902, reproduced by Arno Press in 1968, and also available in various other reprint editions as a print book and an ebook).

> Lester & Gibbs
> Dealers in Groceries, Provisions, Boots, Shoes &
> Wholesale & Retail
> L. & G. having permanently established themselves in Victoria, would respectfully call the attention of Families, Miners and the public generally to their very superior stock, to which they are receiving additions by every arrival
> N.B. – Consignments solicited, and attended to with promptness and dispatch.
> (Kilian, 2020a:42–3)

It was also referred to in the local directory as "Lester & Gibbs, the colored grocers on Yale Street between Whart and Government" (Coles, 2023).[17]

Lester would in February 1860 became the first Black juror in British Columbia. It was not until November 26, 1872, that Blacks were formally added to the jury list. Gibbs would later head up the construction of B.C.'s first railway on the Queen Charlotte Islands, meant to deliver coal from a mine there. As a politician, he would become a town councillor in Victoria in 1866, becoming the first Black elected official in B.C.,[18] was re-elected for a second term, and for a while served as acting mayor. In 1869 or 1870—there is some confusion about the year (Kilian, 2020a:193)—he felt the need to return to the U.S. In his autobiography he wrote:

> It was not without regret that I anticipated my departure. There I had lived more than a decade; where the geniality of the climate was excelled only by the graciousness of the people; there unreservedly the fraternal grasp of brotherhood; there I had received social and political recognition. … Then regret modified, as love of home and country asserted itself (Kilian, 2020a:192 and Gibbs, 1902:109).

In 1892, Lester would likewise sell his property and return to the U.S. Back in the U.S., Gibbs would study law at Oberlin College (where else?),

---

17. For an informative list of works on the subject of the Black history of British Columbia, particularly the Victoria area, go to the online version of this article which has at the end a list of links to other resources.
18. Technically he was the second. Abner Hunter Francis was first elected as a councillor of Victoria in 1865, but he had to resign the day after he was sworn in as he was not eligible, not being listed on the 1863 Assessment Role.

eventually to become the first elected Black judge in America (in Little Rock, Arkansas). In a kind of subtitle for his autobiography, he jammed together, among other achievements, his legal and political career: Attorney-at-Law, County Attorney, Municipal Judge, Register of United States Land, Receiver of Public Monies for U.S., [and] United States Consul to Madagascar" (Gibbs, 1902:1).

In 2016, the city of Victoria made November 19 "Mifflin Wistar Gibbs Day."

James Douglas

We have seen that James Douglas (1803–1877) played a key role in the Black Pioneers coming to British Columbia. His own racial background may have been a factor in this. He was born in British Guiana (now Guyana), out of wedlock, to a woman of mixed race. In an informative biography of Douglas, Julie H. Ferguson writes of his beginnings in the following way.

The story starts with Douglas's mother, Martha Ann Ritchie. Her family was originally from Barbados, and she was the daughter of a white man and a Black mother who was neither poor nor a slave. In British Guiana, women of mixed race like Martha Ann were known as 'free coloured', but how much Black blood ran in James's mother's veins is a mystery. It may have been half-and-half, a quarter, or even an eighth. Both Martha Ann and her mother, Rebecca, could read and write and were businesswomen of some standing in their Guianese community in the early 1800s (Ferguson 2009:15).

He was listed in a Hudson's Bay Company directory—he worked for the company for most of his life—as being 'Scotch West Indian'. He readily passed as white, but his encouraging Black settlers to come to British Columbia at least suggests the possibility of a certain amount of sympathy for people of his maternal line.

There is controversy concerning his being 'Black'. This can be seen in what Wayne Compton wrote in a work focused on the creativity of Black immigrants to British Columbia. He describes Douglas as being "commonly believed to have had African ancestry, a rumour he neither confirmed nor denied," and adds that he is "a figure whose 'Blackness' can only be construed from rumour and speculation" (Compton, 2002). On the other side, the B.C. Black History Awareness Society has written a short biography of James Douglas (https://bcblackhistory.ca/sir-james-douglas/) that supports the view that he is of Black descent.

When he rose to the position of Chief Factor of the powerful Hudson's Bay Company fur trading operation, Douglas faced a struggle in establishing a pro-British definition of the yet undetermined border between British North America and the United States. He was forced to move north when in 1849 the company abandoned Fort Vancouver, where he had lived and worked. It is now part of the state of Washington. He did not want to have to lose his next post in Victoria on Vancouver Island.

One way of doing that was, in his position as the first governor of British Columbia, to encourage as many settlers as possible, of whatever race, to move north to British territory in 1858.

Victoria Pioneer Rifle Corps

Although Douglas was initially supportive of the Black settlers, once they were in British Columbia he pretty much left them to their own devices. An example of this can be seen in the story of the Victoria Pioneer Rifle Corps, otherwise known as the African Rifles. In 1859, under the financial and political sponsorship of the previously discussed Mifflin Wistar Gibbs, it was proposed that a Black militia be formed. This was shortly after no Black men were permitted to join the all-White fire department. The Victoria Pioneer Rifle Corps was formed, the men sworn in by 1861. It was made up of between forty and fifty volunteering Black men, whose purpose was to protect the colony against possible American attack.[19] They were trained by drill sergeants, but were given only ancient flintlock guns as weapons. In her revealing work *City in Colour: Rediscovered Stories of Victoria's Multicultural Past*, which discussed not only Black settlers, but also Hawaiians, Chinese and others who were involved in significant numbers with Victoria's beginnings, May Q. Wong outlined the ways in which Douglas and his successor as governor, Arthur Kennedy, caused the decline in the morale of the Victoria Pioneer Rifle Corps:

> Despite the grave security issues the colony faced, Douglas never did deploy the African Rifles, and by 1863 the group was running short of funds and even shorter on enthusiasm. Members felt betrayed when they were denied the right to participate in Douglas's retirement ceremonies. Too late and too little, they were loaned new rifles to practice drilling for the parade celebrations of incoming governor Arthur Kennedy. They had intended to be his honour guard and escort him to his residence, but were again banned from participating (Wong, 2018:94–5).

In a letter to the editor of the *Colonist*, the Victoria newspaper, on May 9, 1865, Victoria Pioneer Rifle Corps Captain Richard H. Johnson wrote that for the members of the Corps, their

> enthusiasm and ardour as far as this colony is concerned have evaporated. This mean and scandalous manner in which they were treated upon the advent of Governor Kennedy is still fresh in their minds. Having as much human nature under their dark skins as others of a paler hue, they cannot forget the snubbing they received on that occasion (Marshall, 2007).

They would not last long after that.

---

19. Technically, they had one White member who was their bandmaster, who would instruct members of their band. Their band would occasionally perform for the public.

Three Brothers Move to British Columbia: Sophia's Uncles
William Allen "Painless" Jones

William Allen Jones (1831–1897) was the oldest of the three brothers born in Raleigh, North Carolina. As stated earlier, in 1843, not long after his father was attacked viciously by locals retaliating against an anti-slavery speech he had made in New York, the family moved to the free state of Ohio. Like his brothers, William Allen went to Oberlin College. He received his Classical Bachelor of Arts there in 1857. In 1859, along with two brothers, he went to Salt Spring Island, the largest of the Gulf Islands between Vancouver Island and mainland British Columbia, to join in the excitement and promise of the gold rush. He was an effective gold miner, said to have created an "innovative" method of hydraulic mining. This involved "using jets of water to blast hillsides into a slurry from which gold could be extracted" (Kilian, 2020a:108).

In 1862, William ("Billy") Barker discovered gold in the Cariboo[20] region of the western side of the mainland (Wright, 2013:62). The town that would develop there would, predictably, be called Barkerville. It peaked at about five thousand people, but diminished so much after the gold rush that it is now a ghost town that is a historic site.

The population that moved into the Cariboo area was diverse. A rough government count in 1869 gave the following figures:

Race	Males	Females	Total
White	919	69	988
Chinese	720	6	726
'Coloured'	27	4	31
Total	1666	79	1745

(Wright, 2013:54)

Unsurprisingly, the people supervising the count did not include the Indigenous people whose traditional territory this was, the Dakelh or Takulli 'people who go upon the water', a Dene or Athabaskan-speaking people.

Although William Allen seems to have been successful as a miner, he decided to open up a dental practice, advertising himself as "Painless Jones." Dentistry would not have been part of a Classical A.B. education at Oberlin,

---

20. It was so named because of the many caribou that lived there at the time. The name comes from a French version of the Mi'kmaw word qalibu, 'one who scratches' (i.e., in the snow for food).

but there was a dental school in Ohio (see below), one of the first two in the U.S., where he may have received some dental education. Otherwise he would have had to apprentice in the trade:

> In 1825, John Harris, a physician in the Ohio town of Bainbridge, provided medical and dental care for the community. He decided to share his dental experiences with other physicians in southern Ohio. His "school" [opened in 1828] for dental training yielded two colleagues, each of whom was a co-founder of one of the first two formal dental colleges in the world: The Baltimore College of Dental Surgery in 1840 and the Ohio College of Dental Surgery in Cincinnati in 1845 (Ohio State University College of Dentistry, 2023).

William Allen returned to the U.S. in 1865 with the end of the Civil War. According to an article published by the British Columbia Black History Awareness Society, "He visited Oberlin to continue the dental studies he had started earlier" (n.d.). In another article published by that society, it was claimed that he received this dental education at Oberlin College (Hollowell, 2021). While this may be true, I have found no concrete evidence that he did so, the college specializing in what can be called liberal arts. He may have spent some time in Cincinnati, at the dental school there. The first African American to receive such a degree was Robert Tanner Freeman, well named as he was the first person in his family to not be a slave. After receiving two refusals by other dental schools, Freeman became one of six students in the inaugural program in dentistry at Harvard University in 1869.

Wherever he was educated in dentistry, William Allen moved back to Barkerville to become a dentist. On December 1, 1876, he set up his new dental office in what had been, up until 1872, William Rennie's shoe store. It seems that the building may have served another purpose in the intervening years. In his diary, his good friend W. D. Moses recorded that the dental office was in 'Brick top house'. Moses noted also that Brick top was a name used to refer to Hattie Belmont, a young prostitute (Wright, 2013:200).

Concerning William Allen's 'painless' claim, there were available to dentists through much of the nineteenth century three drugs that could have eased the pain of dental work somewhat. These were nitrous oxide (i.e., laughing gas), ether, and chloroform. Perhaps he used one or more of those drugs that would make his dentistry allegedly painless, or at least less painful and worrisome.

If you had a flawed or painful tooth, and went to see Painless Jones, instead of having it removed, you could have it filled with gold, that of course being a readily available substance in the area.

William Allen seems to have been as entrepreneurial in the way that he advertised himself, as was the earlier mentioned Wellington Delany Moses, who also went to Barkerville to set up shop. Moses would run a series of barber shops that he referred to as 'Fashion Saloons'. As stated earlier, he became known as the 'Black Barber of Barkerville'. He claimed to have a 'hair invigorator' that was allegedly a cure for baldness (Wright, 2013:107). This baldness 'cure' would likely be as real as the 'painless' aspect of William Allen Jones' dentistry. Jones and Moses would probably have been fairly close as fellow Black entrepreneurs. That might have been furthered by the fact that a good number of barbers in the nineteenth century augmented their business by extracting teeth. Maybe the two men had conversations on the subject. A measure of their closeness was that William Allen was one of the executors of Moses' will, receiving $138.91 in that will (Afrigeneas Western Frontier Forum).

Painless Jones did not just favour the fortunate folk of Barkerville with his dental skills. There were other towns in the region that lacked resident dentists, so he would visit those towns and provide people with his services. Kamloops was one such town. In a note in a local paper, people were informed of the happy news that "Mr. W. A. Jones, dentist will be at the Dominion Hotel, Kamloops for a short time" (https://twitter.com/kamloopsmuseum/status/1357815866046390273/photo/1).

This was not just a short ride between neighbouring communities. The highway drive between the two locations in the twenty-first century is 485.8 kilometres, or roughly 302 miles.

William Allen Jones's main claim to fame is that he became the first dentist licensed under the British Columbia Dental Act of 1886, obtaining his license on June 26 of that year. Regulated dentistry began in Canada in Ontario in 1867–68. The first dental college in Canada was established in 1875 by the Royal College of Dental Surgeons of Ontario. It became affiliated with the University of Toronto in 1888. William Allen's dental work did not mean, necessarily, that he gave up on gold mining. His response to the 1895 Oberlin alumni office question concerning what he was doing was that he was working in "Gold Mining and Dentistry" (Kilian, 2020a:196).

He would remain in Barkerville for the rest of his life. When he died in 1897 of pneumonia, he was buried in the local Williams Creek Cemetery. He never married or fathered any children.

William Allen Jones's dental office was reconstructed in 1961 in the development of the historic site of Barkerville. This was done with the help of the British Columbia Dental Association, who donated dentistry equipment and offered general advice in the reconstruction of the office.

During Black History Month in February 2023, Barkerville Brewing, based out of nearby Quesnel, B.C., launched a new German style lager beer bearing his name: *Painless Jones Schwarzbier*[21] (Wiebe, 2023).

Left: Painless Jones Schwarzbier (courtesy Barkerville Brewing Co.)
Right: William Allen "Painless" Jones (courtesy Kiddle Encyclopedia, "William Allen Jones Facts for Kids")

John Craven Jones (1834–1911)
Salt Spring Island

John Craven Jones's primary historical significance is based on what he achieved while living on Salt Spring Island, British Columbia. The name Salt Spring refers to springs that are found in the northern part of the island. The current count is fourteen. It is a big island, the largest of the Gulf Islands between Vancouver Island and the mainland. It is roughly 17 miles (27 kilometres) long and from 2 miles (3 kilometres) to 8.94 miles (14.4 kilome-

---

21. The last word can be translated as 'Black beer'.

tres) at its widest, with a total of 83 miles (133 kilometres) of coastline. The tree-covered mountains found throughout the island make it look bigger, and somewhat intimidating when you are crossing the water from Vancouver Island to reach the island, even on a twenty-first century car ferry (I speak from personal experience). The tallest two mountains are Bruce Peak at 709 metres (2,326 feet) and Mount Tuam at 606 metres (1,988 feet).

The island is the traditional territory of the Indigenous peoples known formally as Coast Salish. Archaeological evidence tells us that a number of Coast Salish peoples have harvested the rich plant and shellfish life (leaving the shells behind to make midden layers in the soil), building structures and burying people there for at least four thousand years. They were most likely on the island a lot earlier than that. Significantly, the land rights of these peoples concerning Salt Spring Island remain unceded by treaty to this day.

The Cowichan, one of these peoples, call the island Klaathem, which refers to 'salt'. The second-highest mountain on the island was recorded by Governor James Douglas as 'Chuan' in 1852, a Cowichan word that has been translated as 'straight down to the sea' or 'facing the sea' (Kahn, 1998:11), referring to the drop from the mountain's peak to the seawater. Douglas mistakenly wrote it down as referring to the island itself.

The Saanich, a related people, named the island ĆUÁN,[22] which means 'each end', referring to the fact that there are mountains at each end of the island (Kuam, 1998:11). Its 'official' name during John Craven Jones's time on the island was Admiral Island, given to it by Captain George Henry Richards, to honour Rear-Admiral Robert Lambert Baynes (after whom Baynes Peak is still named). This was changed in 1905 to Salt Spring Island. The Geographic Board of Canada 'officially' wrote the island's name as one word, 'Saltspring', which appears still in some writing. The islanders generally prefer the two-word version: Salt Spring.

While Coast Salish peoples still made extensive use of the island's resources at the time of initial non-Indigenous settlement, a combination of smallpox epidemics in 1769 and 1780, spread by infected Europeans, attacks by the powerful Kwakiutl and Haida, and bullying policies by the settler government reduced, but did not eliminate, the Indigenous presence on Salt Spring Island. The Tsartlip First Nation's reserve (Fulford Harbour Reserve 5) was formally established in 1877; the small (43 acres or 17 hectares) reserve still

22. There is a tradition of capitalizing all the letters in Saanich place names.

exists on the southern part of the island, although no one lives there today (Kahn, 1998:26).

University of British Columbia professor Charles Arnett wrote that there was from the early times of non-Indigenous settlement on Salt Spring Island a kind of convenient myth that there were not any Indigenous people living permanently on the island when the settlers arrived (Arnett, 2016). In actuality, Coast Salish families owned territories in which they had primary rights to hunt and gather to supply them with food, tools and building supplies. These had been passed down over generations.

Marriages between Indigenous women and non-Indigenous men were fairly common. In the census of 1881, it was recorded that of 48 marriages, 13 or 27% were of that combination. In the census of 1891, of 69 marriages, 18 or 26% were (Sandwell 2005:270, footnote 48). It is important to note that the contributions made by the Indigenous women were important to the survival and success of the settlers. As Ruth Sandwell describes it:

> Aboriginal women on Saltspring Island played an important role in teaching their non-Native husbands, families, and neighbours about the environment of Saltspring Island. Memoirs of the early resettlement days note that Native women taught non-Native newcomers to find and prepare the foods and medicinal herbs that sustained generations of their families in the area (Sandwell, 2005:134).

The Story of John Craven Jones

John Craven Jones was born a free Black man on September 10, 1832, in Raleigh, North Carolina, the fourth oldest of the seven children of Allen and Temperance Jones. It seems that he got his second name from his mother's maiden name, which is given on his brother Elias T. Jones's death certificate as 'Craven'. I had previously thought that it had come from Craven County in North Carolina, the state in which he was born, but that is probably incorrect.

Like his five brothers, John Craven Jones received an Oberlin College education.[23] In the academic year 1850–1, at age sixteen, he took courses in the Preparatory Department, achieving marks that earned him acceptance into the college courses. After another five years, he graduated in 1856 with

---

23. There was at least one other graduate of Oberlin living in Salt Spring Island around the time that John Craven Jones did. His name was Fielding Smith (see Kilian, 2020:46 and 48).

a Classical A.B. degree, which involved, among other subjects, proficiency in Latin and Greek, something he would pass on to his students. He then became a teacher and principal at a one-room, one-teacher African-American school in Xenia (not far from Dayton), Ohio, for two years.

John Craven and two of his brothers, Elias Toussaint (the younger) and William Allen (the older), went to Salt Spring Island in British Columbia in 1859. They initially settled on what one author recently described as "the gentle slope leading down to the east side of Ganges Harbour" (Cooper, 2018). This was on the east side of the island, in the northern section of the island. The harbour received that unlikely (to twenty-first century visitors to the island) name as Admiral Baynes had a ship that was called the HMS *Ganges*. John Craven was one of at least thirteen Black men in 1859 with or without families (who were left behind at first) that moved onto the island that year (Sjuberg, 2005). The land may still have had a Black owner in 1881 (Sandwell 2005:165).

He did some teaching that year, but without a school dedicated to that purpose.

In 1861, three major changes took place for John Craven. One was that his two brothers, seduced by the gold rush on the mainland, left to seek their fortune there. That same year he filed his pre-emption papers (Sandwell, 2005:47 and 240, footnote 26) for 100 acres of land in the Vesuvius Bay area (named after the Pacific Ocean sailing ship HMS *Vesuvius* of the Royal Navy, in turn named after the famous Italian volcano), on the northwest coast of the island.

Pre-emption was a serviceable way for early Salt Spring Island settlers who could not afford to pay for their land in advance. The island was the first place in the colony to use such a practice. It was controversial, with Governor Douglas opposing it, wanting payment up front. In an article in the Victoria newspaper, the *British Colonist*, published on June 13, 1859, the conditions of pre-emption of public land were proposed as "on condition of actual residence and the cultivation of a certain number of acres with improvements; and a reasonable period allowed to pay for the land" (as quoted in Flucke, 1951:166).[24]

There were thirty-nine pre-emptions in 1861, twenty-five of which were

---

24. For thoroughgoing analyses of pre-emption see Kahn, 1998:30–32, and Ruth Sandwell's doctoral dissertation "Reading the Land: Rural Discourse and the Practice of Settlement, Salt Spring Island, British Columbia, 1859–1891" (Sandwell, 1997).

later abandoned,[25] nine of which were improved but not purchased, and five of which were both improved and purchased (Sandwell, 2005:66, Table 3.1). John Craven stayed on the land, and earned his improvement certificate by 1872 (Sandwell, 2005:242, footnote 26). By 1874 he (doubtless with help from neighbours, probably including those who had children in one of his two schools) built a house, a barn, some outbuildings (not just an outhouse), cleared the land, and had erected a "large quantity of fencing" (Sandwell, 2005:47). He would have engaged in some farming, but, as one writer notes with probable accuracy, he was "never much of a farmer" (Stratton, 1991). His career was teaching.

Also in 1861, and very importantly for his fellow settlers, he began his more formal teaching career on the island, providing families with an opportunity for their children to receive an education they would not otherwise get, teaching them from grade one to grade eight. The government was not funding any schools on the island at that time. It would be some time before he could pay for the land as part of his pre-emption agreement, as he was not paid by the government during his first ten years as a teacher on the island.

John Craven first formally taught his students in a log house and a shed. In 1861, a log-house school was constructed in Central Settlement, of course situated in the middle of Salt Spring Island, hence its name 'Central School', and another smaller one, a shed, in Fernwood near the northeast shore of the island. The current Fernwood School in the north is close to where the original school was located.

It should be noted that in 1867, there were only nine public schools in all of British Columbia. By 1872, there were five hundred pupils in fourteen public schools in the province, and only sixteen public school teachers.

Original log school house at Central or Vesuvius, c. 1894 (Myrtle Drinkwater and Doris Rogers).
Courtesy Salt Spring Archives (saltspringarchives.com/ Early_Schools/central-school-index.html)

25. According to Sandwell, it was a common practice for would-be settlers to leave the island within a year (Sandwell, 2005:6).

As seen in the picture above, the log-house school appears to have been well-built. Writing in 1969, Bea Hamilton claimed that the original log cabin that was eventually constructed for the northern students had been replaced by a frame building, but the former "still stands close beside it, and is occasionally used for public meetings or Sunday services" (Hamilton, 1969:74).

John Craven would teach three days at one school, then follow that with three days at the other (Kilian, 2020a:139). One of his successors who taught at both schools also did just that in 1878 (McKenzie, 1879:190). One reason that he and the children's parents wanted to have two schools was that the distance between the two schools was roughly five miles (eight kilometres), and the pathways in-between could be dangerous. Students could encounter cougars, bears, and wolves.

John Craven made the long walk himself. He may have done this without his carrying a gun. In Bea Hamilton's *Salt Spring Island*, published in 1969, she claimed that he persuaded other Black settlers not to arm themselves as well as not to retaliate against attacks by Indigenous peoples. Crawford Kilian, novelist and longtime professor at Capilano College, challenged this claim on the grounds of the settlers' need for such weapons for hunting and animal pest control (including the aforementioned cougars, bears and wolves). He also asserted that the latter claim "is based on the legend that the Cowichan people singled out Black settlers for special harassment" (Kilian, 2020a:140). I do not think that the legend is true. But I also believe that John Craven and the other settlers had guns, and would have used them as protection against animal predators in the forested areas.

Were John Craven's schools segregated in the sense of the children of White settlers, Black settlers, and Indigenous people being taught separately? While I have read nothing definitive on the subject, I would think that as John Craven's two schools were the only options available on Salt Spring Island, there would likely be no incentive for parents to withdraw their children from formal education altogether if the schools were not segregated. It should be pointed out that Black, Indigenous, and White students were taught separately in most other parts of Canada at the time, but more choices for exercising prejudice and discrimination were available in those cases.

In 1863, John Craven took a short trip back to Oberlin, Ohio. That same year, he applied to leave his pre-emption land, but nothing seems to have resulted from that.

Several sources make allusions to his being assaulted by other people during his treks to the schools every week, without giving specific concrete examples. Kilian writes, for example, that "Jones was ... being sniped at and occasionally beaten up as he made his rounds" (Kilian, 2020a:149). I am not sure that this actually happened, as I have read no account of any specific case. And you would think that he would at least have asked for protection by the students' parents.

Then there would be the fear brought on by the murders of three Black men in 1867 and 1868 on Salt Spring Island. One, the killing of William Robinson, resulted in a significant court case.[26] In each instance, an Indigenous man was accused of murder. In the Robinson case it was Tom Tshuanahusset, a Penelakut (one of the Coast Salish peoples), who was convicted by an all-White jury and executed. There are two ways in which this relates to John Craven. One involves the fear felt by the Black community on the island during these early years. We see this stated in an article in *The British Colonist* of March 24, 1868: "Many of the colored settlers have their wives and families there, whom they hardly dare leave for a day alone" (as quoted in Sandwell and Lutz, 2000).

Another way in which John Craven was involved in this issue was that he and Scottish-born John Paton Booth, who would later rise to the position of Speaker of the Legislative Assembly of British Columbia in 1898 and serve two consecutive terms in 1900 and 1901, wrote a letter on January 2, 1863, to the Colonial Secretary about who was going to get Robinson's land and other property. They were concerned that Robinson's "heirs" had not been consulted. Their plea for fairness was ignored.

John Craven Finally Gets Paid—But Not Very Much

John Craven did not get paid by the colonial government for the first ten years of teaching, receiving instead farm produce for his meals and help with his farm from the families whose children he taught. Nor was that always easily obtained or forthcoming. In Gail Sjuberg's article, "Salt Spring's first teacher reveals black history lineage," she refers to research done by Saltspring Island resident Arlene Richardson, who uncovered a letter John Craven wrote: "Basically [in the letter] he's making a plea to someone to bring him food, so I knew things weren't all wonderful at that time for him" (Sjuberg, 2005).

John Craven was, however, generally appreciated by the parents of his students. His longevity as their teacher demonstrates that, as does their negative

26. I have seen no evidence that he was related to councillor Henry W. Robinson, mentioned below.

reaction to his being replaced as their teacher. In some other B.C. schools at the time there was a rapid turnover of teachers, and, as we will see later, that situation arose on Salt Spring Island once John Craven was dismissed for no good reason.

It is interesting that, as late as 1868, his occupation was listed as "farmer,"[27] not teacher, in the second Victoria Directory. He did not become a full-time farmer on the island until 1875.

One of the steps to John Craven getting paid for his work as a teacher can be seen in the following official messages:

School Trustees of Salt Spring Island, J. P. Booth, Secretary to the Colonial Secretary, October 26, 1869. Regarding the establishment of a public school with the coloured man, John C. Jones as teacher.

Colonial Secretary's Office to J. P. Booth, Jan. 27, 1870. Approval of appointment of John C. Jones as school teacher (Pilton, 1951:26 and 27).

When the Salt Spring Island School District was established, and John Craven was given official approval, he received his first pay, $40 per month (for every month of the year), with his yearly pay reported as being $500 (Kilian, 2020a:149 and Flucke, 1951:194). His success in finally getting paid was largely due to the support he received from the three-person school board that was the first elected body on Salt Spring Island, one of whose members was Abraham Copeland, a Black settler. In the school board's several communications with the government advocating that John Craven be officially recognized as a teacher and therefore be paid, they referred both to his qualifications, including an American first-class teaching certificate from Oberlin College, and to their need, saying that the settlers had "18 children between the ages of 5 and 16 who are destitute of any opportunity of attending day school" (Kilian, 2020a:19).

However, John Craven was being underpaid, at least in part because of the under-estimation of his qualifications by the Board of Education. In 1872, British Columbia's first non-denominational public elementary system was established. In the First Annual Report of the Superintendent of Education,

---

27. Stratton, 1991:8, stated that John Craven was "never much of a farmer," without giving any evidence. It would probably be because so much of his time was spent preparing classes, marking assignments, teaching, and taking long treks to the two schools where he taught.

published that year, most of the twenty-nine teachers in British Columbia that were listed were recorded as being paid from $50 to $100 per month. Only those teachers who had "temporarily, to end of year" written beside the recording of their pay in the "List of Teachers in the Schools of British Columbia" were paid $40 per month (Jessop, 1872).

That year, John Craven had twenty-five students, eighteen at Central and seven in the north. And there was a new development in education on the island. The community on the south end of Salt Spring Island had enough pupils (ten) to start a school of their own. The teacher sent by the government was not an islander, and undoubtedly White.

John Craven did other work for the community as well. In 1873, he won a seat on the first Salt Spring Island Municipal Council, one of the two Black men—the other being Henry W. Robinson—to serve on the seven-person council.

John Craven Jones Gets Laid Off

In 1872, newly-appointed British-born John Jessop, B.C.'s first Superintendent of Education, whose varied career was not restricted to education (see Dunae, 2003), visited Salt Spring Island to engage in a one-day inspection visit to Jones' class. In his annual report, his description of Jones was quite negative:

> Mr. J. C. Jones is teaching under a temporary arrangement till the end of the year. ... Visited the Island on 27th and 28th June. ... The 28th was examination day, but there were only three pupils in attendance—two girls and a boy. The boy was working in Latin Grammar, having become such a proficient in English Grammar and Geography that those studies were dropped a year ago, and Latin substituted!! So the teacher reported. An examination in those branches and arithmetic did not by any means establish the fact of former proficiency. Teacher's time comparatively wasted by itinerating between the Middle and Northern Settlements. Circumstances do not warrant it, as none of the children are more than three miles from the School house and the road is improving year by year (Jessop, 1876).

Jessop was not classically trained nor as educated generally as Jones. Jessop's post-secondary education, which earned him a teaching certificate, was confined to two six-month programs at the Toronto Normal School in 1853 and 1855. Further, in the "List of Authorized Text Books," there were none for the teaching of Latin (Jessop, 1872).

A number of works have included the following statement, claiming that it appeared in John Jessop's report of 1872. It did not (see Jessop, 1872). Jessop would not have written something so positive about Jones's teaching of those subjects. As yet, I do not know who wrote the following: "The school master offered his charges instruction in Latin, philosophy and human rights education that was the envy of the wealthiest white citizens in nearby Victoria and the mainland" (bcblackhistory.ca/john-craven-jones/ and Hawthorn, 2010).

Influenced no doubt by Jessop's report, the B.C. Board of Education questioned John Craven's capacity to teach. The reason given was that he did not have an official Canadian teaching certificate, a qualification that had only recently been established. To obtain one, he would be required to go to Victoria and write an exam. The local school board argued repeatedly that he should be granted such a certificate based on his Oberlin education and teaching experience in both countries. He had a first-class American teaching certificate, one of the points made by his supporters.

His being both Black and American may have been a negative factor for the probably all-White and Canadian B.C. Board of Education. His being prematurely retired could not relate to any lack of competence or parental approval. The Board dismissed him from his job in 1875. Parents responded by taking their children out of school.

In the Fifth Annual Report of the Public Schools of the Province of British Columbia, we can read that Jessop was quite happy to have John Craven Jones gone and a new teacher, John Britton, replacing him, although, predictably, Britton stayed for only two years. The local support for John Craven was labelled by Jessop as "animosities" and "prejudices," and the new teacher was praised, and offered the promise of a "teacher's residence," something never offered to John Craven:

> I am glad to report a great improvement in school matters in the middle and northern settlement, which constitute this district. Local animosities have subsided; the teacher has overcome the prejudices that existed against him; nearly all the children are enrolled; most of them attending one school or the other, and some of them are going

to both schools. For the first half of the year under review, the attendance was very small indeed, which accounts for the average being only ten. School population is put down at 19, of whom 15 were at school. The irregular attendance was one third, and non-attendance about one fourth.... Visited the school on 7th and 9th March, just at the time when attendance at the middle school settlement was almost *nil*; only three children were present, two of them just beginning to learn. Since re-opening in August, there have been 13 in attendance. The nine pupils, at the northern settlement gave full proof of having made rapid progress during the six months that the school had been in operation, showing that the teacher is industrious and painstaking; that he possesses the faculty of communicating instruction, in a pleasing and efficient manner, was evident to all present on that occasion. A teacher's residence has been proposed, about midway between the school houses. As there is no likelihood of the district being divided, and two teachers employed, for some time to come, this would be a great convenience. Next year's report will, I hope, announce that the suggestion has been adopted (Jessop, 1876:104).

Jessop himself was forced to resign two years later, likely a victim of a change in government. It would be a forced resignation that, based on his treatment of John Craven, he richly deserved.

John Craven taught longer in nineteenth-century Salt Spring Island than did any other teacher. Almost all of the teachers who followed did not stay long, generally one to three years. The exception to that rule was R. A. Purdy, who taught at Vesuvius from 1886 to 1897. John Craven's immediate successors were the following:

John Britton	1875–6
A.C. Howe	1877
Mrs. E. A. Clark	1878–9[28]
S. G. Lewis	1880–1
J. Shaw	1882–5
L. Haskin	1891
(Wellingham, n.d.)	

---

28. For the next few decades, female teachers were much more common than their male counterparts, almost all of them, unlike Mrs. Clark, unmarried.

Education on the island often did not run as smoothly as it had when John Craven was a teacher there. On February 10, 1882, Scottish-born John Patton Booth, several times a Member of the Legislative Assembly in British Columbia, then an educational official, reported to the Superintendent of Education on the firing of the then teacher, probably S. G. Lewis. As recorded by Sandwell:

> In 1882, amidst accusations of racism and political squabbling, the trustees fired the school-teacher and closed the school entirely for a number of months, forcing the third closure since 1875. As the school inspector complained on this occasion, "[h]aving been notified by the trustees that they had dismissed the teacher, and intended to close the school until there was a prospect of better attendance, I visited the school for the purpose of examining it before it closed. Although the teacher's services might have been utilized for a month after the notice of dismissal was given him, the children ceased attending as soon as the fact became known" (Sandwell, 2005:220, see footnotes 125 and 126 on page 293).

Emma Stark

One of John Craven's Black students was California-born Emily Arabella (Emma) Stark (1856–1890). Feeling the fear generated by the three murders of Black people referred to above, the Stark family moved to Nanaimo on Vancouver Island. While there, Emma received her high school education and earned her teacher's certificate. In 1874, at eighteen years of age, she was hired as the first teacher at the Cranberry-Cedar School, making her the first Black teacher on Vancouver Island. Like John Craven, she taught in a one-room schoolhouse, and was paid $40 a month. The house where she lived in Nanaimo has a plaque in front of it that concisely tells her story. She is remembered.

After His Dismissal

Not a lot is known about the years immediately following John Craven's dismissal from teaching on Salt Spring Island. Some writers talk about his farming his land there, most say that he left for Oberlin, Ohio, in the mid-1870s (Kahn, 1998:62 and Kilian, 2020a:196). We know that in 1877 his father Allen Jones was involved with a court case in that city, relating to an Elijah

Tibble. The next year John Craven was also mentioned with respect to that same case.

He was part of the declining Black population of British Columbia, which fell to a figure of 274 as recorded in the census of 1881, fewer than the "Indians," "English," "Chinese," "Scotch," "Irish," "French," "German," and "Welsh," in that order (*Colonist*, May 5, 1885, and Barman, 1991:100).

What he was doing to make a living in the years between 1875 and 1881 is something of a mystery. It would seem that he wasn't teaching, as there is no apparent record of his being affiliated with a particular school during this time. Perhaps he farmed in Ohio. Perhaps he hoped to be able to return to Salt Spring Island to teach. It is interesting that he still had not sold his farm, for which he doubtless received a number of offers. He did not sell it until 1875.

In 1882 he ran as a candidate for the North Carolina Legislature, to represent Enfield, the country seat of Edgecombe County. He did not win.

John Craven Gets Married

When he did sell his Salt Spring Island farm, it no doubt had to do with his getting married. While living in Ohio, he encountered Almira Scott Mitchell (1851–1923), a fellow Oberlin College graduate (1870), who was widowed and left with three young children—Margaret ("Madge"), Edna, and George Henry—with the death of George William Mitchell in 1876. It may well be that their families knew each other. When the president of Oberlin College published his fifty-year retrospective of the college in 1883 and named "the families that came [to Oberlin] early and remained until the later years," the surnames "Jones" and "Scott" both appear (Shipherd, 1883:296–7).

In 1882 John and Almira married—he was forty-eight years old, his wife thirty-one—and he sold his Salt Spring Island property. While I have never read anything about their having children together, in the photograph to the right there are five children, three older and two younger, the latter possibly John Craven's children.

Eventually the family would leave Ohio for Tarboro, North Carolina, set-

(Courtesy Salt Spring Archive, accession no. 2005005002)

tling in the state in which he was born. The first public school in Tarboro was established in 1883. Princeville Graded School (also known as Princeville Graded Colored School) was first established in 1888 as a six-room, six-teacher, six-grade African-American school; it was to be their teaching destination. John Craven, and most likely his wife Almira as well, taught at that school for some years. In 1890 he became the second principal of the school (Knight, n.d.). He taught for eighteen years in the area, presumably at this same school. That would take him well into his seventies.

Princeville is the oldest town incorporated by African Americans in the U.S., established by freed slaves after the end of the Civil War, and incorporated in 1885. In the 2020 census the population was recorded as being 92.66 percent African American (Wikipedia, n.d.).

There is a website whose subject is a still-standing heritage house in Tarboro that is associated with John Craven (at 411 Pitt Street). The website appears to be a little mixed up concerning the dates in which he lived there, but it does show that he lived in a well-built house, and that he is remembered with respect. Here is the text:

> 1 story, L-shaped frame house, beautifully preserved with fine full-width front porch having excellent openwork geometric porch supports characteristic of domestic architecture. A pivotal house in this section of the town. Said built 1870–1875 by builder Jerry Rutledge for a Professor Jones, a black educator, who taught many Tarboro citizens in this era. Jones is described as the second principal of the black public school (https://lib.digitalnc.org/record/236044?ln=en#?c=0&m=0&s=0&cv=1&r=0&xywh=1670%2C1636%2C501%2C304).

There is no way that John Craven was in Tarboro in the first half of the 1870s.

Not long after retiring, he died on December 17, 1911, in Greensboro, North Carolina, where he had lived from at least 1909.

John's step-daughter, Madge Mitchell Falkner/Jones[29] was a teacher as well, becoming head of Guilford County Negro Schools in North Carolina. Her husband, Harry Hall Falkner, became one of the six original teachers at the North Carolina Agricultural and Mechanical College for the Colored

---

29. I don't know whether or not Madge and her brother and sister were ever adopted by John Craven.

Race (founded in 1891), which later became North Carolina A(griculture) and T(echnology), currently the largest historically Black university in the U.S.[30] Both Madge's and Harry's schools were in Greensboro.

It should be noted that three of his nieces—Anna Holland Jones, Fredericka Florence Jones, and Emily Priscella Jones, and, of course, Sophia, who was both teacher and doctor—became teachers as well. They were part of a family that valued education, and it is quite likely that the example of their uncle added coinage to that value.

Salt Spring Island Acknowledges John Craven Jones

John Craven Jones is well remembered on Salt Spring Island. Much has been written about him by Salt Spring Island authors. In 1972, local artist Alfred Temmel painted a mural in John Craven's honour. It could be seen in the Harbour House Hotel at that time. A renovation covered it up with wood panelling. In 2017, it was exposed again, but was beyond repair.

A poet/musician/song writer from the island, Phil Vernon, wrote John Craven's story in song in 2009. The chorus of the poem is:

> You can build your house of timber.
> You can build your house of stones.
> But the best foundation is a good education.
> Said our teacher, Mister Jones.

For the rest of the poem, see https://bcblackhistory.ca/john-craven-jones/.

Another form of remembrance and respect came in an anonymously written (name given as "Soul Dipper") recognition of John Craven's historical contribution to the island's history: "Thank you, John Craven Jones, for all you gave to our Island home" (Soul Dipper, 2012).

Silvia Mangene Alene, the president of the B.C. Black History Awareness Society, was inspired by him when she first came to British Columbia. In an interview in 2023 she spoke of what she felt his legacy was:

> I think his legacy was just that he had been a full member of his pioneer community on Saltspring.... He had found a specialty where he could serve that community. And he did so for a long time, even

---

30. It would graduate its first White student in 1964, and was a major centre of civil rights activism, including its graduate Jesse Jackson.

without payment, essentially out of the goodness of his heart, and the sense that his neighbors' kids needed and deserved an education. He left a legacy of love … he left a legacy of teachings. He left a legacy of respect. He left a legacy of resilience. He left a legacy of humanitarianism—because we all are human, and we all want the same, love and peace (Bauman and Lamport, 2023).

Elias Toussaint Jones (1834–1917)

Elias Toussaint Jones was the third-oldest of his siblings, and the youngest of the three brothers who travelled to British Columbia. He probably was given the middle name "Toussaint" to honour François-Dominique Toussaint Louverture (1743–1803), a leader of the Haitian revolution that gained that country's people independence status from France[31] and who is often referred to as 'the father of Haiti'.

Elias T. graduated in 1859 from Oberlin College. He studied law there, but, although he completed the course, he "never enter[ed] actively into the practice of it." After that, he taught "at various places in Ohio" (National Association for the Advancement of Colored People, 1917:189). This suggests that he might have left for British Columbia at least a year later than his two brothers, who went there the year of his graduation. Elias T. stayed briefly on Salt Spring Island, probably on land pre-empted by his brother John Craven, leaving in 1861 with his brother William for Bakerville to search for gold.

There was a letter sent to him from Oberlin, Ohio, on December 31, 1865. The sender, possibly a family member, did not know Elias' address in Barkerville, or that it had changed a time or two. The letter was addressed to:

Elias T. Jones
Salt Spring Island
Vancouver Island
British Columbia

Added to this, written on a slant on the left side was "In Care of John C. Jones" (Cooper 2018). It appears that Elias T. never received that letter.

In the 1887 Barkerville directory, it is recorded that Elias T. Jones was a

---

31. The name 'Toussaint' is French for All Saints Day. People historically were given that name if they were born on that day (November 1), or in that season. Elias was born in June, so that can't be the source of that name.

miner living in Richfield (Story, n.d.), the latter name being something of an exaggeration as the field was less well-endowed with gold than was Barkerville proper, where some miners went to after not striking it rich in Richfield.

Elias T. did not leave British Columbia until 1892, when he returned (not surprisingly) to the town of Oberlin. The next year, at the relatively advanced age of fifty-nine, he married Blanche Virginia Harris Brooks, then forty-nine (1844–1918). She had received a diploma in Literature as an Oberlin student in 1860, and had become one of the first teachers that the American Missionary Society sent to the southern states. From 1863 to 1867 she would work in Natchez, Mississippi, Henderson, North Carolina, and Knoxville, Tennessee, and engaged in several forms of welfare work as well (Lasser, 2020).

In 1908, Blanche and Elias would both be supporters of the Niagara Movement, the pre-cursor of the National Association for the Advancement of Colored People (NAACP). A meeting of that organization in Oberlin ended with the declaration that they were engaged in "the greatest moral battle of modern times: the fight for the abolition of the color line" (as quoted in Lasser, 2020:1). Elias would eventually become one of the founders of Oberlin's NAACP chapter.

In an Oberlin alumni update in 1895, Elias T. humbly wrote of himself as being a "Gold miner—Since [1892] at Oberlin, Ohio, doing nothing" (as recorded in Kilian, 2020a:125). That was being overly modest. In one of his obituaries it was written that:

> Mr. Jones was a man of excellent habits. Thrift was a passion with him, and though he was severely affected with rheumatism for many years, his garden was enough to put to shame a well man… He was deeply interested in the public questions of the day. He never allowed himself to live wholly in the past, but by reading, and close study kept himself abreast of his time (http://dcollections.oberlin.edu/digital/collection/p15963coll8/id/114).

In another obituary, we read: "He was greatly interested in the work of the National Association for the Advancement of Colored People, and was a member of the same. His death, which took place on May 17, 1917, was felt severely by the community" (National Association for the Advancement of Colored People, 1917:189).

Blanche Virginia Harris Jones (1844–1918)

Blanche Virginia Harris Jones was born in Monroe, Michigan, to free-born parents. She spent her first ten years there until her family moved to Oberlin, her parents clearly wanting their six children to go to Oberlin College. Four of them did, three girls and one boy, including Blanche, who graduated in 1860 at the young age of sixteen. In her "Biographical Sketch of Blanche Virginia Brooks Jones," Carol Lasser writes of her being "a childhood acquaintance" of her eventual second husband. It seems likely that their very similar families knew each other and may have been friends, the eventual spouses knowing each other for years.

Of her first month teaching in Natchez in 1866, along with another female Oberlin graduate, she wrote the following in a letter to the American Missionary Association:

> During this time we had no room to teach in, only going from house to house and teaching fifteen in one place and fifteen in another. I know though our labor was rewarded, not only so far as books were concerned, but in other things, we will never forget those days (Blanche Harris to American Missionary Association, March 10, 1866).

Her eventual brother-in-law, John Craven Jones would have well understood the full meaning of those words, and that situation.

She finally settled for a while in Knoxville, Tennessee. There she married a fellow teacher, William Lafayette Brooks in 1871. They had one child, Maude, in 1872, but she continued her teaching career there, eventually becoming a principal, as did her younger sister Frankie, who had followed an almost identical career path. Her husband William died in 1887.

In 1893, the same year as her marriage to Elias T., she was praised in a three-page section of Dr. Monroe Alpheus Majors' *Noted Negro Women: Their Triumphs and Activities*. It includes the following passage:

> To direct young minds is a task for which Blanche V. H. Brooks is fitted by her natural endowment of taste, judgment, firmness of decision, of character, softened and modified by sweetness of temper (Majors, 1893:31).

In 1896, her daughter (Elias T.'s stepdaughter), Mrs. Maude Brooks Cotton, graduated from Oberlin College. Her granddaughter, Carol Blanche Cotton Bowie (1904–1971), did likewise in 1926. She would eventually earn a Ph.D. at the University of Chicago and work as a psychology professor at what is now the North Carolina Central University.

In 1913, the year Blanche turned sixty-nine, she was a very active member of the all-Black/all-female Mutual Improvement Club in Oberlin, Ohio. Among other functions, she was mentioned in the yearbook of that organization under the heading "The Chairman of Committees, as the Chair relating to 'school'" (Anonymous, 1913). While all the members were women, Blanche was still consistently referred to as "Mrs. Elias Jones," more of a custom then than now.

In an Oberlin College publication, we find a picture of Blanche as a teenager, no doubt when she had graduated with a diploma from the Literary Course, at age sixteen, in 1860. (Courtesy Oberlin College Archives, Popular Images, ohio5.contentdm)

Two More Uncles Plus an Aunt of Sophia Jones
Charles Brougham Jones (early 1830s–1925)

Charles Brougham Jones was given his second name in honour of Henry Brougham, a liberal British politician who as a member of Parliament promoted legislation against slave trading. Charles studied at Oberlin College from 1847 to 1849, but did not graduate. From 1849 until 1852 he was a seminary student. Despite his non-graduation, Charles did rather well as an educator.

At some point he moved to Brooklyn, Illinois, not far from St. Louis. The town is often known as 'Lovejoy', after the White abolitionist and Presbyterian minister Elijh P. Lovejoy, who was assassinated in 1837. Lovejoy/Brooklyn was primarily an African-American community, referred to as 'America's First Black Town'. Jones married Jane Gibbs,[32] and they had six children.

From his first days there he was successful. He early on received a job as a teacher at the Lovejoy School, and was soon, at twenty-two, chosen to be the principal. He also became the local tax collector. He achieved his most prominent job when he became mayor in 1903.

In his definitive study of the town, *America's First Black Town: Brooklyn, Illinois 1830–1915*, Suniata Keita Cha-Jua tells the reader of the significance of Jones being a mayor to which no scandal could attach:

> Charles Jones became mayor during a critical moment in Brooklyn's history. The mayor and street commissioner had been incarcerated, and William Doug West Jr., the town clerk and a schoolteacher, had been driven from public life in disgrace. Less than two months after Jones's election, the man he had replaced as principal of Lovejoy School, David F. Wyatt was lynched (Cha-Jua, 2002:190).

Charles B. Jones endeavoured to be a model of morality in his time as mayor. Again to quote Cha-Jua:

> During his first year in office, Mayor Charles B. Jones launched an offensive against prostitution. Like many middle-class 'race men and women,' Jones probably feared the activities in the saloons, gambling, and jook joints undermined the moral fiber of the community and created circumstances that could provoke an attack by Brooklyn's white neighbors (Cha-Jua, 2002:198).

As Cha-Jua notes, it should be seen that Charles' "offensive" was directed primarily against prostitutes openly parading outside (and inside) the saloons and other like places. There was relatively little done to close down

---

32. I do not know whether she was any relation to Mifflin Wistar Gibbs, discussed earlier in this chapter. I have found no evidence that she was.

the places where the prostitutes were found. These were typically owned and operated by well-to-do Black men who were peers of the mayor. This is not to blame Jones, just noting the likely restrictions placed on Jones in trying to make significant changes and, instead, just removing the disreputable 'female window dressing' from around the premises.

We know that he financially profited from his various undertakings. The headline of his obituary, published in the *Toledo Blade* of May 5, 1925, read "Mayor Leaves Estate at $300,000."

His son, Charles Jr. would follow in his father's footsteps, first becoming a teacher, and later becoming mayor of Brooklyn, Illinois.

James B. Jones (1839–1894)

James B. Jones was the youngest son of the family, being born in 1839. He seems also to be known by the name 'Junius'. He attended Oberlin College, not graduating but leaving at the end of his junior year. This was not unusual at the college. Of the first hundred Black students attending the college in its first thirty years, only thirty-two completed their degrees. Still, like so many others in his family, he became a teacher, as probably did many others who received some valuable education at that institution while not graduating. He married and fathered one child. He died in Kentucky, and was buried in Oberlin. Unfortunately, I could not find any specifics concerning his teaching or anything else about his life.

Bethany Jones

The one sister in the family was called Bethany, a name derived from a place found in the Bible. She was the second oldest of the siblings, born in 1824. In the 1850 Census we see that she was living with her parents and her siblings. In the 1880 Census she was recorded as living on her own, no doubt never marrying, just like her nieces, brother James Monroe's four daughters. In 1894, she was living with her brother Elias T. Jones and his wife. In one Oberlin College source, there is a sentence that mentions the graduation dates of her four brothers, but ends with "Bethany, the only sister, did not finish her education" (Bigglesworth, 2002). This could mean that she spent a year or more at Oberlin College, but did not complete a program. She did have a trade, however, becoming an engraver, possibly working with her brother James 'Gunsmith' Jones' in so doing (see the discussion in chapter one of whether it was a sister or daughter who worked with him).

Summary

We can safely say in sum that the Jones family one generation ahead of Sophia was well-educated and ambitious, setting good examples for Sophia and her siblings. She was following a family tradition of beating the odds against being Black in Canada and the United States during the era in which they lived.

References

Alene, Silvia Mangue, n.d, "The Importance of Including Black History in B.C Curricula and Heritage Programming."

Anonymous, 1894 "JONES – At Lebanon, Ky., Nov. 28th 1894, of pneumonia, James B. Jones." *The Oberlin News*, December 13.

Anonymous DigitalNC, nd., "John Craven Jones Home, 411 Pitt St., Tarboro, NC.

Anonymous, 2005+. "He taught for 10 years without pay: John Craven Jones, Salt Spring Island's First Teacher," Community Stories: BC's Black Pioneers: Their Industry and Character Influenced the Vision of Canada, B.C. Black Awareness Society, https://www.communitystories.ca/v2/bc-black-pioneers_les-pionniers-noirs-de-la-cb/story/he-taught-for-10-years-without-pay-john-craven-jones-salt-spring-islands-first-teacher/

Anonymous, n.d., https://bcgenesis.uvic.ca/saltspring_island.html?hi=baynes_rl

Anonymous, n.d., https://lib.digitalnc.org/record/236044?ln=en#?c=0&m=0&s=0&cv=0&r=0&xywh=1029%2C-1591%2C3616%2C5590

Anonymous, n.d., https://museum.bc.ca/wp-content/uploads/2021/02/279-Spotlight-Black-History.pdf

Anonymous, n.d., https://www.canadianmysteries.ca/sites/robinson/images/view.php?id=-1943&lang=en&size=2

Anonymous, n.d., "Saltspring Island's First Teacher," saltspringarchives.com/education/usha/JCJonesU.htm

Anonymous, n.d., https://www.communitystories.ca/v2/bc-black-pioneers_les-pionniers-noirs-de-la-cb/gallery/john-craven-jones-schoolteacher-immortalized-in-1972-mural/

Anonymous, "John Craven Jones with his wife Almira (Scott) Jones" (1885), https://www.communitystories.ca/v2/bc-black-pioneers_les-pionniers-noirs-de-la-cb/gallery/john-craven-jones-with-his-wife-almira-scott-jones-1885/

Anonymous, https://www.communitystories.ca/v2/bc-black-pioneers_les-pionniers-noirs-de-la-cb/gallery/john-craven-jones-with-his-wife-almira-scott-jones-1885/

Anonymous, John Craven Jones, Teacher (photograph of mural on the wall of the Ganges Pub, Salt Spring Island).

Arnett, Chris, 1999, *The Terror of the Coast: Land Alienation and Colonial War on Vancouver*

Island and the Gulf Islands, 1849–1863 (Vancouver: Talon Books).

-----, 2016, "Indigenous History of Salt Spring Island," *Salt Spring Exchange*, https://saltspringexchange.com/2016/02/03/indigenous-history-of-salt-spring-island/

Barman, Jean, 1991, *The West Beyond the West: A History of British Columbia* (Toronto: University of Toronto Press).

Bauman, Martin, and Jackie Lamport, 2023, "Salt Spring's first school teacher: Black BC history and a legacy of love," *Capital Daily*, February 28.

Baumann, Roland, M., 2010, "Constructing Black Education at Oberlin College: A Documentary History", Athens, Ohio, Ohio University Press, p. 86, ttps://ohio5.contentdm.oclc.org/digital/collection/photos/id/366/

B.C. Black History Awareness Society, n.d., "Earliest Pioneers (1858–1899), Emma Stark," https://bcblackhistory.ca/emma-stark/

-----, n.d., "Earliest Pioneers (1858–1899), John Craven Jones," https://bcblackhistory.ca/john-craven-jones/

-----, n.d., "Earliest Pioneers (1858–1899), William Allen Jones," Stories bcblackhistory.cawilliam-allen-jones

Bigglesworth, William F., 2002 (revised edition), "They Stopped in Oberlin: Black Residents and Visitors of the Nineteenth Century," Oberlin College.

"Black Canadian Scientists to Know," Sciencerendezvous.ca/news/2021/02/25/black-canadian-scientists-to-know/

Blanche Harris to American Missionary Association, March 10, 1866.

CBC, 2016, "Salt Spring Island's black settlers set stage for today's community: Former Salt Spring resident Evelyn C. White explores the island's black history," February 3, https://www.cbc.ca/news/canada/british-columbia/salt-spring-island-black-1.3433086.

Cha-Jua, Sundiata, 2000, *America's First Black Town: Brooklyn, Illinois, 1830–1915* (University of Illinois Press).

Coles, Sidney, 2023, "How a pair of shoes kickstarted Black history in Victoria," *Capital Daily*, December 10.

Compton, Wayne, ed., 2002, *Bluesprint: Black British Columbian Literature and Orature* (Arsenal Pulp Press).

Cooper, Tracy, 2018, "Early Mail from the U.S. to Salt Spring Island," December, *British Columbia Postal History Newsletter,* vol. 27, no. 4 (whole no. 108), pp. 1093–4.

Coquitlam Heritage, n.d., "Black Settlers in B.C." https://www.coquitlamheritage.ca/black-settlers-in-bc

DigitalNC, nd., "John Craven Jones Home, 411 Pitt St., Tarboro, NC."

Dunae, Patrick A., 2003 "Jessop, John," *Dictionary of Canadian Biography*, vol. 13, University of Toronto/Université Laval, http://www.biographi.ca/en/bio/jessop_john_13E.html.

"Elias T. Jones Dies at his Home Sunday. Respected Colored Man Was Graduate of Oberlin," collections.oberlin.edu/digital/collection/p15963coll8/id/114

Encyclopedia of B.C. Preview: Go Do Some Great Thing: Chapter Nine: "They are uncrowned kings," https://www.knowbc.com/limited/Books/Go-Do-Some-Great-Thing/Chapter-Nine

Fawcett, Edgar, 1912, *Some Reminiscences of Old Victoria* (Toronto: William Briggs).

Ferguson, Julie H., 2009, *James Douglas: Father of British Columbia* (Toronto: Dundurn Press).

Flucke, A. F., 1951, "Early Days on Saltspring Island," saltspringarchives/publications/FluckeEarlyDays.pdf

Gallher, Bill, 2011, *A Man Called Moses: The Curious Life of Wellington Delaney Moses* (Touchwood Editions).

Gibbs, Mifflin Wistar (1902, rpt. 1968), *Shadow and Light: An Autobiography with Reminiscences of the Last and Present Century* (Arno Press).

Hamilton, Bea, 1969, *Salt Spring Island* (Vancouver: Mitchell Press).

Harris, Carolyn, 2020, "Syvia Stark," *The Canadian Encyclopedia*.

Hawthorn, Tom, 2010, "The youth of tomorrow get a taste of Vancouver Island's past," *The Globe and Mail*, March 4.

"He taught for 10 years without pay: John Craven Jones, Salt Spring's First Teacher," Island'scommunitystories.ca/v2/bc-black-pioneers_les-pionniers-noirs-de-la-cb/story/he-taught-for-10-years-without-pay-john-craven-jones-salt-spring-islands-first-teacher/

Hollowell, Shay, 2021, "Scholarship in memory of Jerry Macdonald," Friends of Barkerville, *Cariboo Goldfields Historical Society Newsletter*, vol. 20, no. 2 (Fall/Winter).

https://bcblackhistory.ca/sir-james-douglas/

https://dcollections.oberlin.edu/digital/collection/p15963coll8/id/114

https://lib.digitalnc.org/record/236044?ln=en#?c=0&m=0&s=0&cv=0&r=0&xywh=1029%2C-1591%2C3616%2C5590

https://museum.bc.ca/wp-content/uploads/2021/02/279-Spotlight-Black-History.pdf

https://www.canadianmysteries.ca/sites/robinson/images/view.php?id=1943&lang=en&size=2

https://www.communitystories.ca/v2/bc-black-pioneers_les-pionniers-noirs-de-la-cb/gallery/john-craven-jones-schoolteacher-immortalized-in-1972-mural/

https://twitter.com/kamloopsmuseum/status/1357815866046390273/photo/1

https://www.knowbc.com/limited/Books/Go-Do-Some-Great-Thing/Chapter-Eleven

https://www.communitystories.ca/v2/bc-black-pioneers_les-pionniers-noirs-de-la-cb/gallery/john-craven-jones-with-his-wife-almira-scott-jones-1885/

Irby, Charles C., 1974, "The Black Settlers on Saltspring Island in the Nineteenth Century," *Phylon*, vol. 35, no. 4, pp. 368–74 (Clark Atlanta University).

Jessop, John, 1872, *First Annual Report of the Superintendent of Education*, August 30.

-----, 1876, *Fifth Annual Report of the Superintendent of Education.*

"John Craven Jones with his wife Almira (Scott) Jones (1885)," https://www.communitystories.ca/v2/bc-black-pioneers_les-pionniers-noirs-de-la-cb/gallery/john-craven-jones-with-his-wife-almira-scott-jones-1885/

"John Craven Jones, Teacher" [Photography of mural on the wall of the Ganges Pub, Salt Spring Island].

Jones, Jayne Lloyd, n.d., "30 Things You Will Love About Salt Spring Island," in *Island Information Book, Salt Spring Accommodation Group*, www.saltspringaccommodation.ca

https://curric.library.uvic.ca/homeroom/content/schools/public/firstann.htm

Kahn, Charles, 1998, *Salt Spring: The Story of an Island* (Harbour Publishing).

Kilian, Crawford, 2008, "BC's Amazing Black Pioneer: Why Mifflin Gibbs still matters today," *The Tyee*. February 7.

-----, 2020a, *Go Do Some Great Thing: The Black Pioneers of British Columbia* (Harbour Publishing).

-----, 2020b, "The Case of Archy Lee," pp. 7–15, https://www.aclunc.org/sites/goldchains/explore/archy-lee.html.

Knight, Rudolph (in part), n.d., North Carolina Association of Black High School Alumni, n.d., https://ncabhsa.com/clients/875427/File/Program.pdf

Lasser, Carol, 2020, "Biographical Sketch of Blanche Virginia Harris Brooks Jones," *Biographical Database of Black Women Suffragists*, updated 2022.

Majors, Monroe Alpheus, 1893, *Noted Negro Women: Their Triumphs and Activities* (Jacksonville, TN: M. V. Lynk Publishing House).

Marshall, Valin G., 2007, "Victoria Pioneer Rifle Corps (1861–1865)," *B.C Black Historical Awareness Society*, https://bcblackhistory.ca/victoria-pioneer-rifle-corps/

McKenzie, C. C., 1879, "Supplementary Report," January 22, saltspringarchives.com/reports/docs/1879.pdf

McWhirter, R., 1988, "A Brief History of School District #64," Canadian Education: A History, July 25, http://saltspringarchives.com/reports/docs/McWhirt001t.pdf

Moore, Shirley Ann Wilson, *Sweet Freedom's Planning: African Americans on the Overland Trails 1841-1869.*

National Archives, Milestone Decision, n.d., "Dred Scott v. Sanford (1857).

National Association for the Advancement of Colored People, 1917, "An Alumnus of Oberlin" in "Men of the Month," p. 189 in *The Crisis: A Record of the Darker Races*, vol. 14, no. 4, https://www.marxists.org/history/usa/workers/civil-rights/crisis/0800-crisis-v14n04-w082.pdf

"'Painless Jones'—The Barkerville Dentist," Community Stories—BC's Black Pioneers: Their Industry and Character influenced the vision of Canada, https://www.communitystories.ca/v2/bc-black-pioneers_les-pionniers-noirs-de-la-cb/story/painless-jones-the-barkerville-dentist/

Petersen, Hanna, 2022, " 'Painless Jones': B.C's first dentist was a Black miner from Barkerville," *Prince George Citizen*, February 13.

Pilton, James William, 1951, "Negro Settlement in British Columbia 1858–1871," dissertation for Master's Degree, Department of History, University of British Columbia.

Quesnel Observer Staff, 2020, "Wells artist prints portrait of B.C.'s first dentist," October 17.

Rautenbach, Usha, 2012, "Central School, John Craven Jones," http://saltspringarchives.com/Early_Schools/central-school-john-craven-jones.html

Rogers, Brittany, 2009, "Saltspring Island, British Columbia," *Blackpast*.

Salt Spring Island Foundation, 2022, https://ssifoundation.ca/cfc-toolkit/

Sandwell, Ruth Wells, 1997, "Reading the Land: Rural Discourse and the Practice of Settlement, Salt Spring Island, British Columbia, 1859–1891," doctoral dissertation, Department of History, Simon Fraser University.

Sandwell, Ruth and John Lutz, n.d., "Who Killed William Robinson: Race, Justice and Settling the Land," *Great Unsolved Mysteries in Canadian History*, https://www.canadianmysteries.ca/sites/robinson/murder/19thcentury/2323en.html

Sjuberg, Gail, 2005, "Salt Spring's first teacher reveals educated black history lineage," *Gulf Islands Driftwood*, February 23.

Soul Dipper, 2012, "Celebrating Black History Month of February," Word Press, February 1.

Story, Wanda, nd., "Barkerville Directory" sites.rootsweb.com/~bccarobp/barkerville1887.html

Stratton, Morton B., 1991, "History of Agriculture on Salt Spring Island: Farms, Farmers and Farming 1859–1885, August 15, https://saltspringmuseum.com

Wellingham, John, n.d., "Early Schools on Salt Spring," https://saltspringarchives.com/reports/docs/JohnWellingham.pdf

Wiebe, Joe, 2023, "Quesnel's Barkerville Brewing has brewed a special bear in honour of BC's first licensed dentist William Allen 'Painless' Jones," February 9, 2023, BC Ale Trail, https://bcaletrail.ca/barkervilles-painless-jones-schwarzbier-celebrates-black-history-month/

Wikipedia, 2023, "Ohio State University College of Dentistry," April 30.

Wikipedia, n.d., "Princeville, North Carolina," https://en.wikipedia.org/wiki/Princeville,_North_Carolina

Wikitree, n.d., "Margaret c.v. Madge, (Mitchell) Faulkner (abt. 1874–1838), wikitree.comwiki/Mitchell-37160

Wong, May Q., 2018, *City in Colour: Rediscovered Stories of Victoria's Multicultural Past* (Touchwood).

CHAPTER FOUR

Sophia and Other "Firsts"

Before I tell the story of Sophia Bethena[33] Jones (pictured above), I want to set out the sociological and historical context of her achievement in terms of how long it took in Canada for Black males and White English Canadian and French Canadian women to become doctors, for Black and Indigenous women to become nurses, and for the first Black Canadian female to become

---

33. The name 'Bethena' is uncommon and somewhat mysterious in meaning and origin. I could find only a little information about it. In the nineteenth century it could be found as a family name in England, and in the southern states of South Carolina and Tennessee. I suspect that it has biblical origins, and comes from the Hebrew language.

a lawyer. Added to that will be a bit of the story of the first Black man to become a mailman in Toronto; even that seemingly small advance was difficult for the individual to achieve. As with Sophia, the struggles these people went through were very similar, the achievements hard won, and important social progress was made with their success.

First Black Canadian Male Physicians

Establishing who was the first Black male Canadian doctor involves a unique research trap which does not seem yet to be resolved. The best treatment of this situation that I have read is in Frank Mackey's 2018 article "1848, 1861, 1926—Which Came First?"[34] The year 1926 pertains just to McGill University, and refers to Jamaican-born Kenneth Melville (1902–1975). The 1848 date also involves a McGill claim. But there is also the 1861 claim involving the University of Toronto, the medical school that turned down Sophia when she applied.

The American First Black Doctor: 1839

In the U.S., the first Black medical student to graduate was Samuel Ford McGill (1815–1871),[35] who was born in the U.S. and raised in the then American colony of Liberia in western Africa. He had difficulty at first finding a school that would accept him, but he graduated in 1839, from the Dartmouth Geisel Medical School in New Hampshire (Green, 2020).

The 1848 Graduate

Dr. William Wright graduated in medicine from McGill University at twenty years of age in 1848. He was born in Quebec City in 1827, and had a Black father and a White mother. In the census of 1861, he identified himself as being Creole. In the 1901 census, he referred to himself as Black.

A number of articles identify him as the first Canadian-born Black doctor (Lurie, 2022, Mackay, 2018 and 2020, and his great-great niece Sandra Stock, 2018, who discovered her Black heritage through a genetic test).

After Wright graduated, he worked as an assistant to a doctor for the next few years, at some point becoming a surgeon and obstetrician. In 1853 he began teaching at McGill as well as being the Chair of the Department of

---

34. He also wrote *Done with Slavery: The Black Fact in Montreal, 1760–1840*, published by McGill-Queen's University Press in 2010.
35. This is not a mistake, just a strange coincidence.

Materia Medica (Pharmacy). In 1882, when he was fifty-five, his students complained that he was not keeping up to date with the latest developments in medicine. It was a time when medicine was advancing, but that student complaint was probably racially related to a significant extent. The students felt strongly enough about him that they boycotted his classes. He retired in 1883. Black medical teachers in the U.S. sometimes received this kind of treatment because of their race. That could have been a significant factor in what was going on in Wright's case as well.

Fortunately, Dr. Wright had another career that he could fall back on to a certain extent. In 1864 he had been ordained as a deacon[36] of the Anglican Church, upgraded to the position of priest in 1871.

The 1861 Graduate

The 1861 graduate was Dr. Anderson Ruffin Abbott (1837–1913) who, unlike Sophia, was accepted as a medical student at the University of Toronto. His parents (Wilson Ruffin Abbott and Ellen Abbott) were freed slaves who had become relatively well-to-do, owning a general store and other valuable properties in Mobile, Alabama. But their situation became dangerous following what is known as Nat Turner's Rebellion of 1831 in Virginia, which involved the killing of fifty-five to sixty-five White Americans, the deadliest slave revolt in American history. Wilson Abbott was warned of potential danger, which was followed by the burning down of the family general store. They ended up in Toronto in 1835. At that time the city had about 9,300 residents, roughly 500 of them Black. Wilson Abbott initially ran a tobacco shop, but it eventually failed. He turned his hand to real estate, and was a success. In 1840, he was elected to Toronto city council, the first Black Canadian elected to office. In 1876, the year of his death, he owned forty-two houses, plus other properties. Anderson's parents could well afford a university education for their son.

Dr. Abbott's education involved several innovative institutions. It began at the Buxton Mission School in a Black community by that name near Chatham, also called the Elgin Settlement (see appendix). It was initially an all-Black school, but its obvious quality led parents of White children to apply as well. Within two years it became the first racially integrated public school in North America, with 250 students. An article in the *Bulletin of the American*

---

36. A deacon is an ordained minister in the Catholic, Anglican or Orthodox Church, having a position lower in rank than that of priest.

*Left: Dr. Abbot in 1863 in uniform.
Right: In later life.
(Courtesy
Toronto Public Library)*

College of Surgeons describes it as being the "Original 'Pipeline' of Black Surgeons" (Nakayamo, 2022) similar in a number of ways to Oberlin College in offering educational opportunities to Black students. Its existence may well have been one of the factors that gave Sophia Jones the idea that a Black person could become a doctor.

What should not be considered unusual by those who have read the previous chapters of this book is that Abbot's education later included studying at Oberlin College, in the Preparatory Department in 1856–7. This was followed in 1857 by his studying chemistry at University College in Toronto, and then, in 1858, admission to the Toronto School of Medicine, receiving his medical degree in 1861.

Dr. Abbott was aided in his career path by the African American Dr. Alexander Thomas Augusta (1825–1890), who was admitted to the medical program at the University of Toronto sometime during the 1850s and who received his Bachelor of Science in Medicine in 1860. In a reversal of what happened to Sophia, Dr. Augusta had been turned down by American medical schools before he was accepted at the University of Toronto. This points to gender working against Sophia.

Dr. Abbott, although Canadian, joined the Union Army in 1863 (he and Dr. Augusta were two of eight Black doctors to do so), where he became a decorated war hero. He also worked as a doctor at the Freedmen's Hospital in Washington, which was founded in 1862 as the first American hospital dedicated to serving freed slaves. Dr. Augusta would be in charge there, becoming in that way the first African-American hospital administrator in U.S. history.

Abbot met with President Abraham Lincoln, who was impressed by him. When Lincoln was shot on April 14, 1865, Abbot was one of the doctors who attended to him. Upon Lincoln's death, his widow gave him the plaid shawl that Lincoln had worn on the way to his inauguration in 1861.[37]

Abbott was discharged from the U.S. Army at the end of the Civil War in 1865. He returned to Canada, opening up a medical practice in Chatham. In 1874, he became the first African Canadian to be appointed as coroner, serving in that position in Kent County.

He would later live with his family and set up his medical practice in three different southern Ontario locations: Dundas in 1881, Oakville in 1889, and Toronto in 1890. The main reason for these moves is not clear (see Slaney, 2003:73). Perhaps he encountered some resistance in one or both of those locations. In Dundas, along with his successful medical practice, he became the assistant editor of a magazine, writing under an alias in articulating his criticisms of racist views. Maybe racists in that town discovered his hidden identity and made life tough for him there.

Abbot would definitely not have liked the name Dundas, the town being named after Henry Dundas, a Scottish politician who significantly delayed the abolition of the Transatlantic Slave Trade in Britain in the 1790s by getting an amendment passed saying essentially that the abolition be "gradual" rather than immediate. In the summer of 2020, an online petition calling for the renaming of Dundas Street in Toronto was signed by close to 14,000 members of the public, and on July 14, 2021, Toronto City Council voted in favour of renaming the street and other civic properties that bear Dundas's name. A Community Advisory Committee was formed of Black and Indigenous leaders plus people living and working along Dundas Street businesses. Its task was to develop a shortlist of alternative names for the street. On December 23, 2023, Toronto City Council approved renaming Yonge-Dundas

---

37. This shawl was passed down through successive generations of the Abbott family until the mother of author Slaney, not knowing its history, gave it to an American cousin, who donated it to the Wisconsin Historical Society in Madison, Wisconsin.

Square Sankofa Square,[38] as well as renaming both the Dundas and Dundas West subway stations in 2024 and 2025 respectively (the Dundas station serves Toronto Metropolitan University, formerly Ryerson University, named after a historic racist), but directed staff to "pause" renaming efforts for the street itself.

In 1894, Abbott moved to Chicago, where he became first the surgeon-in-chief, then, in 1896, the Medical Superintendent of Provident Hospital, also in Chicago. It was a training hospital for African American nurses. In 1897 he returned to Toronto.

His eldest son, Wilson Ruffin Abbott II, born in Chatham, became a doctor like his father, going to the University of Toronto and Cornell University, and graduated in Pharmacy and Medicine at the University of Illinois. He would eventually benefit medicine by developing an innovative way of treating tuberculosis involving the collapsing of the lung. It should be noted, that he married a Florence Nightingale, but not the famous one.

In 2002, Dr. Abbott was recognized as one of the University of Toronto's "Great Minds" honorees, with a banner tribute on a lamppost at the main campus. Both Abbot and Augusta were honoured with plaques unveiled at the University of Toronto downtown campus on February 8, 2023.[39]

Now an obvious question: why is there no consensus as to his being the first Canadian-born Black doctor? I have no good answer to that question. Does it relate to provincial parochialism or the competitive nature of two of Canada's oldest and best-known universities? I cannot say for sure, but Wright is the one that I would choose for the honour, even though my doctorate was awarded to me by the University of Toronto, and I was born and raised in that city.

First Female Physicians in Canada
Margaret Anne Bulkley/James Barry (c. 1790–1865)

The person who was probably the first female physician[40] to practice medicine in Canada comes with a very strange tale. There is a lot of speculation

---

38. This comes from a term used in Ghana referring "to the act of reflecting on and reclaiming teachings from the past which enables us to move forward together" (Casaletto, 2023). The Dundas station will be renamed after Toronto Metropolitan University (TMU), the new name for Ryerson, with consultations being held on a new name for the Dundas West Station.
39. For a discussion of the Abbot family history, as well as Black life and institutions in southern Ontario during the nineteenth century, I highly recommend the book written by Dr. Abbott's great-granddaughter, Catherine Slaney, *Family Secrets, Crossing the Colour Line*, 2003, Dundurn Press.
40. Of course, Indigenous women in Canada practiced medicine for thousands of years before the time of first contact, and continue to do so without the official title 'physician'.

here. The standard story is that this doctor was born in Ireland and recognized as being female, bearing the name of Margaret Anne Bulkley. The next part has her identifying herself as James Barry, the name of a relative, disguising herself as a male so that she could be admitted to the much-acclaimed medical school at the University of Edinburgh. After graduating, the person now known as James Barry enlisted in the British Army and received a good number of promotions until coming to Canada in 1857 as the Inspector General of Hospitals, the highest rank a doctor can achieve in the army. She died in 1865, and reputedly asked to be buried with her clothes on, with no preparation of the body. This did not happen. A female servant took off her clothes and claimed that 'he' was a 'she'. This has been much discussed with one popular theory that soon developed being that Margaret Ann Bulkley was a hermaphrodite. We might use the term intersex today. We do not know for sure that she was intersex or just a female who disguised her sex really well.

Emily Stowe

The first female Canadian physician to practice medicine with a formal degree in Canada was Emily Howard Jennings Stowe (1831–1903). She was born in Norwich, Ontario, where today there is an elementary school named after her. Her path to becoming a medical professional was a long one. She taught elementary school for seven years starting at age fifteen. In 1853, she applied to study medicine at Victoria College in Cobourg, but they turned her down as she was a woman. She then went to the Provincial Normal School for teacher training for a year. Upon graduation, Emily accepted an appointment to be a principal at an elementary school, the first Canadian woman to become one.

Like Sophia Jones, Emily Stowe was later denied entry at what was then called the Toronto School of Medicine in 1865. She then decided to move to the U.S. to study at the New York Medical College for Women, graduating in homeopathic medicine in 1867. Homeopathic medicine, developed in Germany several decades earlier, was a form of medicine that was originally based on two fundamental theories. One is that 'like cures like', the homeo- in the word meaning 'similar to'. This theory hypothesizes that a disease can be cured by a substance that produces similar symptoms in healthy people. The other foundational theory is 'the law of minimum dose', the idea that the lower the dose of the medicine, the greater effectiveness it has as a cure.

Emily Stowe's two youngest sisters would also graduate in medicine there in 1875. To receive an official license in Ontario, she had to take a full course in a recognized Canadian medical school. It was still not easy for a woman to find such a place. Finally, in 1870–1, along with Scottish-born Jennie Trout (1841–1921), who would become the first 'recognized as being female' licensed doctor in Canada in 1875, she was accepted at the Toronto School of Medicine. Neither completed the program there due to strong and obnoxious opposition from both male students and at least one professor.

She did not give up on medicine, however, working as a physician's assistant, until she finally received her Canadian medical license from the College of Physicians and Surgeons of Ontario in 1880, making her the second female Canadian to become a licensed doctor. In 1883, wanting to create physician opportunities for other women, she founded the Ontario Medical College for Women in Toronto, which eventually became Women's College Hospital, a prominent teaching hospital. In 2018 she was inducted into the Canadian Medical Hall of Fame. There is a summer student research program in her name, funded and run by the Women's College Research Institute, along with the Centre for Wise Practices in Indigenous Health, that provides career developing opportunities for students who are "Black, Indigenous, racialized, gender diverse (queer, trans, two-spirit, non-binary), and/or living with a disability" (*Muskrat Magazine*, 2022).

Ann Augusta Stowe-Gullen

Ann Augusta Stowe-Gullen (1857–1943), the eldest daughter of Emily Stowe, born in Mount Pleasant, Ontario, was the first Canadian woman trained in Canada to become a physician. She had been accepted at the Toronto School of Medicine (affiliated with Victoria College that became part of the University of Toronto) in 1879 at age twenty-two; this was the same school that had rejected her mother's application back in 1853. Ann Augusta graduated in 1883. Three more female doctors would graduate in 1884 at Queen's University based in Kingston. From 1885 until 1893 there would be twenty-three more (Brearly, n.d.).

Irma Le Vasseur—First Female French Canadian Doctor

Irma Le Vasseur (1877–1964) was the first female French Canadian physician. Like Sophia Jones, she had to go to the U.S. to be accepted in a school of medicine. She graduated in 1900 from the School of Medicine at Saint Paul University in Minnesota. She then worked in New York for a few years.

Returning to Quebec, she petitioned for a private member's bill entitling her to work as a doctor in her home province. In 1903, it was passed and she became the twelfth woman in Quebec, and the first French Canadian woman, to earn the right to practice medicine in the province. The others were English. She worked in France and Germany, then returned in 1906 to Quebec, where she became the first French Canadian woman to actively practice medicine in that province. That same year she co-founded the first pediatric hospital in Quebec, the Hôpital Sainte-Justine in Montreal, of which she was a director. In 1908 she was relieved of that position, the reason not being clear in the literature.

She would move back to New York, staying there until 1915. After that she worked in Europe for a while, then she returned to New York to work for the Red Cross. In 1922, she went back to Quebec, where she was involved with founding two more pediatric hospitals.

There was relatively little recognition for her pioneering work while she still lived. However, in 2009, a sculpture of her was erected in Quebec City. In 2018, she was designated a historic figure by the Ministère de la Culture et des Communication du Québec.

First Non-White Nurses
Black Nursing Firsts

The first nursing training facility in Canada was the General and Marine Hospital in St. Catharines, Ontario, which opened in 1874. In the U.S., the first nursing school, the New England Hospital for Women and Children, opened in 1872. African American Mary Eliza Mahoney (1845–1926) was the first Black woman to graduate from that program in 1879.

It would be some sixty-six years before the first Black Canadian woman graduated from a nursing program. Bernice Redmon, from Toronto, had to go to St. Philip Hospital Medical College in Virginia, to achieve her career goal, as she was rejected by Canadian nursing schools. She graduated with a nursing diploma in 1945. That same year she returned to Canada and was hired by the Nova Scotia Department of Health, the first Black nurse to practice in public health. Later she became the first Black woman appointed to the Victorian Order of Nurses in Canada.

In 1948, two women, Ruth Bailey from Toronto and Gwennyth Barton from Halifax, graduated from the Grace Maternity School of Nursing in Halifax. In 1950, Marissa Scott, from Owen Sound, Ontario, became the first

Black woman to graduate in and practice as a nurse in Ontario. In 1954, Clotilda Douglas Yakimchuk was the first Black woman to graduate from the Nova Scotia Hospital School of Nursing in Halifax. Her work as nurse and mentor earned her, among other honours, the Order of Canada and the Order of Nova Scotia.

Two comments are to be made here. First, Canada was a lot slower to allow Black nursing students than the U.S., contrary to what many Canadians might think (and I might have thought prior to doing this research). Second, the names of the first such students in the U.S. are much easier to find than the fact Sophia B. Jones became the first female Black Canadian doctor.

Charlotte Edith Anderson Monture—First Indigenous Canadian Registered Nurse

Becoming a non-White nurse was not just difficult for Black women. The same was true for their Indigenous counterparts. Charlotte Edith Anderson Monture (1890–1996) was a Mohawk (Kanien'kehá'ka 'people of the flint') of the Six Nations First Nation in southwestern Ontario. She became the first Canadian Indigenous woman to become a registered nurse. After being turned down by nursing schools in Canada, she went to New York to be educated in the profession at the New Rochelle Nursing School, graduating with a degree in 1914. She was first in her class. She began her career in the city as a private school nurse. When the U.S. entered World War I in 1917, she volunteered to serve in France in the U.S. Army Nurse Corps. In that year, the Canadian government passed the Military Voters Act of 1917. This included giving the federal vote to women who were army nurses in the war. This made Edith Monture the first female Status Indian and registered band member to have the federal vote in Canada. She would have been 'enfranchised,' losing this kind of status if she had received a university degree in Canada. To understand something of the significance of this, Status Indians/registered band members did not have the federal vote without losing their status until 1960. And losing that status could well mean losing the right to live on the reserve you were born on, as well as other rights.

After the war, Edith returned to her home community, where she worked as a nurse and a midwife in the hospital on the reserve. It would be fair to say that she assisted in the birth of most of the tribal citizens of several decades.

There is no great certainty as to who was the first Native American registered nurse. Elizabeth Sadoques Mason (1897–1985), an Abenaki, who graduated from the nursing program at Mary's Free Hospital for Children, in New York in 1919, is often presented as being the first (Morris 2021), but her sister, Maude Sadoques, may have preceded her. In the words of Maria Dintino: "It is presumed Maude earned her nursing degree around 1914 and it is known that Elizabeth was awarded hers in 1918 since the certificate still exists" (Dintino, 2023). Lula Owl Gloyne (1891–1985), a woman of Cherokee and Catawba heritage, graduated from the nursing program at Chestnut Hill Hospital in Philadelphia in 1916, so she may have been the first.

Albert Jackson: Toronto's First Black Mailman

In July, 2017, a plaque was erected to celebrate the achievement of Albert Jackson, a Black man who became the first Black mailman on May 12, 1882, a job which he kept for thirty-six years. His family, like so many others, had escaped to Canada on the Underground Railroad. On the plaque, we read that: "Because of racial discrimination, white postal workers refused to train Albert to deliver mail, so his supervisor assigned him to an indoor position as a hall porter instead (Howells, 2017)." In addition, a "heated debate ensued in the press about his appointment," but fortunately, Prime Minister John A. Macdonald wanted the support of Black voters, so he supported Jackson's appointment.

In May 2022, a new, technically innovative zero-carbon parcel facility in northeast Toronto was named after Albert Jackson.

Violet Pauline King Henry—A Legal First

Violet Pauline King Henry (1929–1982), who was born in Calgary and was a descendant of one of the first Black families (the King family) to move to Alberta, was the first Black woman to practice law in Canada. It was something that she had wanted for a long time: "Her Grade 12 yearbook caption read 'Violet wants to be a criminal lawyer' " (Ruck, 2017). She went to the University of Alberta, where out of 142 students in the Faculty of Law, she was one of only three women. She received her Bachelor of Laws in 1953 and was called to the Alberta Bar in 1954, the first Black person to do so. This was so much considered an achievement by Black people in the U.S. as well as Canada that the International Brotherhood of Sleeping Car Porters and Maids, organized and run by African Americans, had their president go to Calgary to make a special presentation to her to mark her achievement.

Her brother, Ted King, was not a lawyer, but in his position as president of the Alberta Association for the Advancement of Coloured People, he launched a legal challenge (no doubt aided by his sister) against a Calgary motel's racially discriminatory policy in 1959. The case made it all the way up to the Supreme Court of Alberta, but was not successful. In the words of a biographer, "King's case exposed legal loopholes innkeepers could exploit in order to deny lodging to Black patrons" (Ruck, 2017). In 2000, Alberta passed the Alberta Human Rights Act, which included an end to such discrimination. In November 2018, staff in an Edmonton hotel violated that law by preventing two Black and two Middle Eastern young men from staying there (St. Onge, 2018).

Sophia Bethena Jones (1857–1932)—First Canadian Black Female Doctor
Sophia Bethena Jones was born on March 16, 1857, in Chatham, Ontario, a town that was a major northern terminus of the Underground Railroad, known in the 1850s as the 'Black Mecca of Canada', a name now used in the Black Mecca Museum run by the Chatham-Kent Black Historical Society. Consequently, the town had a relatively large Black population when Sophia was growing up, making up at least a third of the local population.

Her early education would have been in a segregated private school, not funded by the province, but financially supported by the local Black community, with Black teachers. In 1850, the government of what was then called Upper Canada (later Ontario) passed the Common Schools Act. There was a Separate Schools Clause that allowed for the establishment of separate schools for Catholics, Protestants and Black people. The Common School Trustees used this clause to support the practice of racial segregation (Henry-Dixon, 2021). Black separate schools were the only options available for Black students in Chatham until 1891, later in other communities in the area (Smith, 2004).

The last Black separate school in Ontario closed in 1965. This was achieved to a significant extent because of the efforts of newly elected Liberal MPP Leonard Braithwaite, the first Black Canadian to be elected to provincial legislature. In his initial speech to the Ontario Legislature on February 4, 1964, he spoke out against the part of the Common Schools Act that allowed for racial segregation of Black students. A month later, the Conservative education minister introduced a bill that amended the Act. It passed.

Sophia went to Wilberforce Collegiate Institute, which, among its other functions, prepared Black students for university. For the significance of the name 'Wilberforce', see the discussion below.

She must have done well in those schools, as she was accepted as an undergraduate at the University of Toronto in 1879. She was ambitious, wanting to become a doctor like the Black doctors who practiced medicine in Chatham when she was growing up. However, she was not admitted to the medical school there as she was doubly damned by being both a woman and Black. In comparison, a White woman born a year earlier than her would eventually practice medicine in Chatham. This was Mary Louise Agar, who graduated from the University of Toronto Medical School in 1890.Chatham-Kent Physician Tribute, https://ckphysiciantribute.ca/doctors/mary-louisa-agar/).

Another White woman, Dr. Sarah Jane Carson, who would also eventually practice medicine in Chatham, was born in 1865, graduating from the University of Toronto Medical School in 1889, and practicing medicine in Chatham from that year until 1933.

Opposition to Women Medical Students and Blacks at Queen's University

Women generally had a difficult time applying to medical school in Canada from the late nineteenth century until well into the twentieth century. For example, the Royal College of Physicians and Surgeons in Kingston, which was the forerunner of Queen's Faculty of Medicine, responding to pressure from male students and at least one male professor, banned female students from being accepted in 1883. The ban lasted until 1943. Female students already enrolled were segregated from their male counterparts. Kingston Women's Medical College, loosely affiliated with Queen's, was formed in 1883, but only lasted until 1894.

In 1918, the University Senate at Queen's University voted to ban the further enrollment of Black students in its medical program. There were about fifteen Black men in the program at the time. While they were not kicked out, mockery (e.g., the White student performance of a stereotypical minstrel show) and general pressure caused about half of them to leave. It wasn't until 1965 when Black students were once again enrolled in the program at Queen's. As we have seen, that was when the law was changed in the province. There was no official repeal of the school's own ban. It was just ignored. Perhaps the administrators did not want that racist aspect of the university's history to have attention drawn to it. It wasn't until 2018, a century after the university's ban, that it was officially repealed. This was followed by a formal apology in 2019, as well as teaching about the existence of the ban in the medical curriculum, and the introduction of scholarships for Black medical students (Glauser, 2020).

I think that it can be said that no medical school in Canada was historically completely free from prejudice against students such as Sophia B. Jones.

Potential Black Physician Role Models for Sophia Jones

When Sophia Jones was being educated in Chatham, local Black doctors served as role models and would likely have influenced her career choice, even though most of them were only in Chatham for a short time. The one with potentially the greatest influence would have been the aforementioned Dr. Anderson Ruffin Abbott, who had graduated from the medical school affiliated with the University of Toronto, and who practiced medicine in Chatham from 1866 to 1881, when Sophia Jones was growing up.

There were Black doctors other than Abbot in Chatham who could have influenced her, even if only for a short time. One was Michigan-born Dr. Amos Array (1829–1886), who, following his graduation in Cincinnati in 1855, moved to Chatham, and had a medical practice there until he left for the U.S. during the time of the Civil War. That influence may have been minimal, as she was a small child when he left.

Dr. Martin Delany (1812–1885) is another possible role model. He does not seem to have graduated from the Harvard Medical School, White student resistance being a force to reckon with for the Black medical students there. However, he set up practice in Chatham in 1856, staying three years, and later becoming a notable writer and political activist both in Liberia[41] and the U.S.

Spending less time in town was Dr. Samuel C. Watson (1832–1892), who first went to Oberlin but did not graduate. In 1853 he went to the University of Michigan, not finishing the program there. Finally he studied at the Western Homeopathic College in Cleveland in 1856 before obtaining his license in 1857. He practiced medicine in Chatham for about a year, got involved with the gold rush in British Columbia, then returned for a year or two, only to leave to practice medicine in Toronto, then to run a drug store in Detroit.

Finally, there was Kentucky-born Dr. Robert Maxwell Johnson (1826–1871), who was accepted at the prestigious University of Edinburgh Medical School, paying in part for his tuition with lectures he would give on Black slavery. He received his degree in 1871, and moved to Chatham in 1871. Tragically, he died there that fall.

---

41. Liberia was established early in the nineteenth century in western Africa by African Americans who believed they would have more freedom and prosperity in Africa than they would in the U.S. In 1847, Liberians declared their independence as a country. The United States did not fully recognize their independence until 1862. The Liberian flag looks just like an American flag, but with just one star.

Chatham-Kent Physician Tribute

The lives of these Black physicians, and the lives of physicians in Chatham-Kent generally, are well described on a very useful website: Chatham-Kent Physician Tribute, https://ckphysiciantribute.ca. There is also a tribute to Sophia on the website, even though, unlike all the others so honoured, she never served as a doctor in Chatham. She was not one of the doctors mentioned on the site until I suggested that she be included. The editor was quick to agree.

In sharp contrast to the number of Black male physicians working in Chatham during the nineteenth century, the first Black woman to practice as a doctor in Chatham was Dr. Avril Marie MacDonald, born in Kenya in 1962. She served as a doctor there from 1986 to 2015.

Sophia B. Jones's Educational Success

After teaching for a year, Sophia took a chance and pursued her dream. She was accepted at the University of Michigan Medical School in 1880, and on May 16, 1885, at twenty-eight years of age, she became the first Black woman to graduate from that program. This was twenty-one years after the first African-American woman, Rebecca Lee Crumpler, graduated as a doctor in 1864 at the New England Female Medical College (see Rothberg, 2020–2, https://www.womenshistory.org/education-resources/biographies/dr-rebecca-lee-crumplerfor her biography).

The University of Michigan Medical School has honoured Dr. Jones in a number of respectful ways. There is the Sophia Jones Lectureship on Infectious Diseases, and the Sophia B. Jones Room is used for conferences. Then there is the Fitzbutler Jones Alumni Society, named after her and the first Black male graduate of the medical school, William Henry Fitzbutler, who graduated in 1872. It was formed in 1997 to support Black students and alumni. On the webpage of the NMF Fitzbutler-Jones Alumni Society of Michigan Scholarship Fund we read the following:

> Established in 2019, this need-based **$5,000** scholarship will be awarded to a **first-, second-, or third-year African American student who is enrolled at the University of Michigan Medical School for the coming academic year**, and who has demonstrated excellence in academics and financial need (https://nmfonline.org/scholarships/nmf-fitzbutler-jones-alumni-society-of-the-university-of-michigan-scholarship-fund/; emphasis in the original text).

Sophia's Career

The newly graduated Dr. Sophia B. Jones went rather rapidly from the University of Michigan Medical School to teaching at what would become Spelman College, the oldest historically Black college for women, located in Atlanta, Georgia. It was founded in 1881 as the Atlanta Baptist Female Seminary, with classes first taught in the Friendship Baptist Church. It was given the name Spelman to honour three longtime antislavery activists, Harvey Buel and Lucy Henry Spelman and their daughter Laura Spelman Rockefeller, wife of John D. Rockefeller, the latter contributing significant funding to the school. Spelman was from its foundation a school just for women, and still is today. Most of the students have always been African Americans.

Sophia joined the faculty in 1885 as the first Black female teacher, teaching there until 1888. In 1886, she was involved with the founding and operating of the nursing program. (For information about her time and influence there see Spelman College, 2016, "Sophia B. Jones Charts a Course of Success for African-American Doctors," *Our Stories*, April, and 2020, "Dr. Sophia B. Jones and Ludie Clay Andrews, Class of 1906," *Our Stories*, April.)

She went on from there to teach at Wilberforce University, in Xenia, Ohio, a private institution dedicated to the education of Black students. It was named after British politician William Wilberforce, who led the movement to abolish the slave trade with the Slave Trade Act of 1807, and to abolish slavery itself, with the Slavery Abolition Act of 1833. On its website Wilberforce University refers to itself as "the nation's oldest private, historically black university, owned and operated by African Americans. Its roots trace back to its founding in 1856."

She continued her career elsewhere, first in St. Louis, where she probably worked again in Black nursing education. No information appears to be readily available about her time there. She later worked at the Frederick Douglass Hospital in Philadelphia, which was an African American institution that provided the first training school for Black nurses in the city, as of 1895, the year of Douglass' death. Douglass (1817-8–1895) was born a slave in Maryland, escaped when he was about twenty, and became a major abolitionist, social reformer, and politician as well as a brilliant orator and a prolific writer.[42]

In 1903, Sophia practiced medicine in Kansas City, Missouri. In the De-

---

42. He wrote three autobiographies, *Narrative of the Life of Frederick Douglass, an American Slave* (1845), *My Bondage and My Freedom* (1855), and *Life and Times of Frederick Douglass*, 1881 and 1892.

cember 18, 1903, edition of *The Rising Sun*, there is a summary of her career to that point, reproduced to the right. It also contains two references that I do not completely understand. One refers to "her removal," relating to her leaving the Douglass Hospital. I have the sense that it was not her choice in the matter. The other reference is to her being without a hospital to work at in Kansas City, instead working out of her home, and doing "office work for the present."

> Dr. Sophia B. Jones, a graduate of the medical department of the University of Michigan, is enrolled among Kansas City's physicians. Dr. Jones has had much experience, having been resident physician in Spellman Seminary, Atlanta, where she established the first Nurse's Training School in the South, and also in Wilberforce University. She was until her removal to Kansas City, on the staff of Douglass Hospital, Philadelphia. She may be found at 1213 Bellefontaine avenue, where she will do office work for the present. Office hours, 10 to 12 a. m., 4 to 6 p.m.

A 'Bulletin' of Oberlin College dated March 31, 1905, indicates Sophia's older sister, Anna Holland Jones, was living at that address too. Anna would later live on her own in a neighbourhood where she and the rest of the Black population would encounter strong prejudice (see the discussion of Anna's life in the next chapter).

Judging from a fairly recent advertisement for its sale (https://www.redfin.com/MO/Kansas-City/1213-Bellefontaine-Ave-64127/home/93132169), her two-storey house at that address is still standing, but probably not for very long. It looks like it is falling apart. It is deemed "off market" and the vacant 7446 square foot vacant lot behind it had an estimated cost of $27,476.

Dr. Sophia the Inventor

Sophia's abilities went beyond those of practicing medicine. She was also an inventor. On July 15, 1890, she filed her patent notice for an invention of hers, a new-and-improved barrel trunk (that being a large trunk, typically with a curved lid):

> Be it known that I, SOPHIA B. JONES, a citizen of the United States, residing at Atlanta, in the county of Fulton and State of Georgia, have invented a new and useful Barrel-Trunk, of which the following is a specification. This invention relates to barrel-trunks, or that class of

trunks which are constructed in the shape of a barrel for the purpose of enabling them to be conveniently handled without danger of breakage; and it consists in certain improvements in the details of construction of the same, which will be hereinafter fully described, and particularly pointed out in the claims (Jones, 1890).

She wrote about her invention's unique features and its advantages over previous barrel trunks, including the following:

[T]he operation of my invention and its advantages will be readily understood from the foregoing description, taken in connection with the drawings hereto annexed. When the trunk is in use, the feet may be readily placed in position, and the trunk will thus be sustained in an upright position. When the trunk is to be transported, the feet may be quickly detached and packed within the trunk, thereby avoiding the danger of their being broken in transit (Jones, 1890).

There is a series of pictures of Sophia's barrel trunk in her patent notice (https://patents.google.com/patent/CA34906A/en).

You might be wondering, as I still do, what the connection might be between Sophia's medical work and the 'new and improved' barrel that she invented. While there might be such a connection, strictly speaking, there does not necessarily have to be. She grew up with a father, James Monroe Jones, who was a skilled tradesman, and a younger brother George Allen Monroe Jones (1863–1944), who became a carpenter (see next chapter).

Dr. Sophia the Writer

Sophia also was a gifted writer. We can see this in an often-cited article she wrote on the subject of Black medical history. In September 1913, Sophia published an article entitled "Fifty Years of Negro Public Health" in *The Annals of the American Academy of Political and Social Science*. At the time she was the resident physician at the Agricultural and Mechanical College in Greensboro, North Carolina, later to become a branch of the University of North Carolina. Not surprising is the fact that this article was one of the first research publications by a Black female doctor in the medical field. My writing about her needed to include her own words, speaking her views. So here are three passages from the article:

> In the course of the past fifty years the Negro race has had to contend against the hostile forces of ignorance, poverty and prejudice while adjusting itself to the new conditions imposed by the life of freedom, and consequently its mortality rate has been excessively high, due largely to pulmonary tuberculosis and infant diseases; but now a marked improvement is apparent, and its mortality rate is declining with that of the general population (Jones, 1913:145).

Her ever-generous heart credited a broad variety of people who contributed to lowering the Black mortality rate:

> Within the last five years attention has been directed specifically toward the reduction of the high death rate. Negro physicians and teachers, some enlightened pastors, graduates of literary and industrial schools, are all united in the determined efforts they are making to reduce the Negro death rate, especially the death rate from tuberculosis. Splendid assistance and generous cooperation have been extended by white physicians and public health officers, who, by lectures to schools and churches are emphasizing, as never before in the history of the nation, the importance of public health to the Negro (Jones, 1913:142).

She ended the article by writing as a leading community figure, educator, and health professional, setting out an optimistic view of her race in terms of the intersection of the three fields during the next fifty years:

> The need of the hour, so far as Negroes are concerned, is for systematic and organized effort directed at the problem of sanitation and public health in all colored schools and colleges, in all churches and communities, in fraternal societies and in private families. It is not too much to expect for a race which, in fifty years, has reduced its illiteracy from and estimated percentage of 95 to one of 33.3 as given by the census figures of 1910. Let the teaching of general elements of physiology, including sex physiology, and sanitation be placed on a rational basis in all colored schools and colleges, in the hands of men and women thoroughly trained and with full knowledge of the health problems named above[43] and there can be little doubt that the issue of the conflict will

---

43. Those would be tuberculosis, infant mortality, and venereal disease.

be such a rapidly declining death rate and reduced morbidity as will astonish the civilised world (Jones, 1913:146).

It is a shame that Sophia never wrote a book, and that I have not been able to find anything else that she wrote. It seems likely to me that she published more material that would enlighten myself as well as other readers about her ideas were.

Retiring in Monrovia

Sophia eventually moved from Kansas City to Monrovia,[44] California, which was physically but not completely socially linked to Los Angeles. There had been an African American community there since the 1880s. By the 1910s, it was essentially a segregated community of African and Mexican Americans that lived literally on 'the other side of the tracks' from other, White-dominated sections of Los Angeles. They had to cope with "White Trade Only" signs in L. A. stores and restaurants, and with being hired by others only to do menial jobs.

Judging by the information presented in her obituary—that she had lived in Monrovia for fifteen years and practiced medicine for thirty-seven—she would have moved there in 1917. She possibly practiced medicine there out of her home, until her sister moved in with her in 1921 and together they ran what *The Michigan Alumnus* of 1920–1921 (p. 255) referred to as an "orange ranch." I am assuming from the use of the word "ranch" that it was a commercial enterprise, and knowing the abilities of both Sophia and her sister Anna, I am willing to bet that it probably was a successful venture. She died on September 9, 1932, about six months after her sister. They were buried in the same cemetery, the Live Oak, in Monrovia, where her three sisters and brother George Allen were and would be buried. It was a segregated cemetery. Desegregation generally did not take place in Monrovia until the 1960s.

Obituary in the Monrovia News-Post, *September 10, 1932*
FORMER PHYSICIAN DIES AT HOME HERE

Miss Sophia Bethnia [sic] Jones M.D., died yesterday at home, 1301 South Shamrock avenue. She was born May 16, 1857 in Chatham, Ontario, Canada. She had lived in this country for fifty years and in Mon-

---

44. Apparently this was not named after President James Monroe, but after William N. Monroe, a railroad construction engineer who purchased much of the land and laid out the town in the early 1880s.

rovia for 15 years. She had practiced medicine and surgery for 37 years. She is survived by one brother, George A. M. Jones and one sister, Miss Emily of Monrovia.

Funeral services in charge of Remaker company will be held tomorrow afternoon at 2 o'clock from the A[frican]. M[ethodist]. E[piscopal]. Zion Church. Interment will be made in Live Oak cemetery.

Her Monrovia house has been demolished, and was replaced by a smaller building that currently (2023) houses a fire damage restoration service.

Her reputation lives on, and does honour to her family and to the history of Black people in both Canada and the United States. She still needs to be better known as a Canadian who succeeded against the odds, one of the main messages of this book. She should be considered, officially, a Canadian of Historic Significance, something which has yet to happen.

I have found a short piece written about her by the Hope Clinic in Michigan with the heading, "Black History Month: Dr. Jones and Improving Medical Care." Sadly, I have seen nothing like that in any Black History Month commentary in her homeland of Canada. There definitely should be. She was Canadian born, raised, and educated prior to university. The Black community of Chatham educated her, made her strong during that time, and enabled her to see that becoming a doctor, despite her race, was definitely a dream that could come true.

She needs to be recognized for her achievements both home and abroad, in the country of her birth and youth. This recognition is slowly beginning, in a short piece about her, along with six other "Black scientists" on CBC Radio: "Meet 7 groundbreaking Black scientists from the past: Innovators across disciplines who have made significant, enduring contributions to the world" (2021), and John Rhodes's article "Chatham-born doctor helped nurses training program in Atlanta" (*Chatham-Kent This Week*, 2021). But that recognition still has a very long way to go.

Appendix: Nineteenth-Century Buxton

Buxton (also known as the Elgin settlement) was established in 1849. Like the larger settlement of Chatham it was one of the last stops on the Underground Railroad. On the website of the Buxton National Historic Site and Museum, they include a very positive statement coming from an American government official, Dr. Samuel Gridley Howe, who in 1863 was sent to investigate the conditions of freed slaves both in the southern states and in Ontario. He was quite positive about the advances made by the Black settlers in Buston. A similar description could also hold for the Chatham of the time:

> There are signs of industry and thrift and comfort, everywhere; signs of intemperance, of idleness, of want, nowhere. There is no tavern and no groggery; but there is a chapel and a schoolhouse. Most interesting of all are the inhabitants. Twenty years ago, most of them were slaves who owned nothing, not even their children. Now they own themselves; they own homes and farms, and they have their wives and children about them. They are enfranchised citizens of a government which protects their rights. They have the great essentials of human happiness, "something to love, something to do, and something to hope for" and if they are not happy it is their own fault (https://www.buxtonmuseum.com).

References

Anonymous, 1903, "Sophia B. Jones working at Kansas City," *The Rising S[u]n*, Kansas City, MO, December 18, https://www.newspapers.com/clip/9264268/sophia-b-jones-working-at-kansas-city/

Anonymous, 1914, "Fund Raiser," *The Kansas City Sun*, Kansas City, MO, October 1914, p. 1.

Anonymous, "William Wright, first person of colour to earn a medical degree in Canada," McGill-Bicentennial, https://200.mcgill.ca/history/william-wright-first-person-of-colour-to-earn-a-medical-degree-in-canada/

Anonymous, 1932, "Monrovia News" (Sophia B. Jones obituary), *California Eagle*, Los Angeles, October 7, p. 4.

Anonymous, 1944, "George Allen Jones" (his obituary), *Monrovia Daily News*, March 9, p. 2.

Anonymous, 1921, *The Michigan Alumnus*, vol. 27, October 1920–August, 1921, Alumni Association of the University of Michigan.

Anonymous, n.d., https://windsormuseum.ca:8080/mwebcgi/mweb.exe?request=record;id=31594;type=101).

Anonymous, 2016, "William Wright became the First Black Medical Doctor in British North America," https://ua.ssmu.ca/2016/08/31/william-wright-becomes-the-first-black-medical-doctor-in-british-north-america/

Binning, Margaret B., 2008, *Manassas Industrial School Personnel 1894–1938: Faculty, Staff, Students and Graduates; Partial Listing*, Ruth E. Lloyd Information Center (RELIC), Bull Run Library, Manassas, VA.

Binning, Margaret B., 2008, *Manassas Industrial School Personnel 1894–1938: Faculty, Staff, Students and Graduates; Partial Listing*, Ruth E. Lloyd Information Center (RELIC), Bull Run Library, Manassas VA.

Bonner, Claudine, 2014, "Nina Mae Alexander: Daughter of Promise," in *The Promised Land*, pp. 91–105.

Brandice, Nelson, "Paul Quinn College," *Waco History*, accessed May 19, 2022, https://waco-history.org/items/show/79.

Bristow, Peggy, 1994, " 'Whatever you raise in the ground you can sell it in Chatham': Black Women in Buxton and Chatham 1850–65", *'We're Rooted Here and They Can't Pull Us Up': Essays in African Canadian Women's History*, pp. 69–142.

Buxton National Historic Site & Museum, n.d., https://www.buxtonmuseum.com

Calkins, Laura M., 2013, "Jones, Sophia Bethena," *Oxford African American Studies Center*, March 15.

Chatham-Kent Physician Tribute, n.d., https://ckphysiciantribute.ca

CityNews, 2022, "Canada's First Two Black Doctors—U. of T. Alumni—To Be Honoured with Plaques Near St. George Campus," May 26.

Dintino, Maria, 2023, "Elizabeth Sadoques Mason: One of the First Native American Nurses in the United States," May 2, *Nasty Women Writers*.

Fryer, Mary B., 1990, *Emily Stowe: Doctor and Suffragist* (Toronto and Oxford: Hannah Institute and Dundurn Press, Canadian Medical Lives, No. 6).

Glauser, Wendy, 2020, "When Black medical students weren't welcome at Queen's", *University Affairs*.

Green, Susan, 2020, "Grit and Determination", *Dartmouth Medicine—The Magazine of the Geisel School of Medicine at Dartmouth*, Spring.

-----, 2023, "Geisel School of Medicine Dedicates Samuel Ford McGill Lounge in Honor of First US Black Medical Student Graduate," *Geisel School of Medicine*, February 13.

Gwiazada, Emily, 2008, "James Barry", *The Canadian Encyclopedia*, January 20, last edited August 17, 2021.

Hauch, Valerie, 2018, "Canada's first Canadian-born Black doctor got his MD license in 1861," *Toronto Star*, February 8.

Henry-Dixon, Natasha, 2021, "Racial Segregation of Black Students in Canadian Schools," *The Canadian Encyclopedia*, August 30.

Howells, Laura, 2017, "New plaque celebrates Albert Jackson, Toronto's first black postman," *The Toronto Star*, July 21.

https://www.findagrave.com/memorial/239805320/anna-holland-jones/photo

https://kclinc.org/blackhistorystories/

Jefferies, Keisha, 2020, "Recognizing history of Black nurses a first step to addressing racism and discrimination in nursing, *Dal News*, Dalhousie University, May 13.

Jones, Anna H, 1911 Letter from Anna H. Jones to W. E. Du Bois December 18, 1911, https://credo.library.umass.edu/view/full/mums312-b006-i298

Jones, Sophia B., 1890, "Barrel Trunk", *United States Patent Office*, January 18.

-----, 1912, "Fifty Years of Negro Public Health," *The Annals of the American Academy of Political and Social Science*, pp.138–146.

Kennedy, Brendan, 2023, "Canada's first Black doctors honoured with plaques," *Toronto Star*, February 9.

Lesmond, Joan, 2006 "Celebrating Black Nurses this February and Beyond," *Registered Nurse Journal*, https://rnao.ca/sites/rnao-ca/files/Celebrating_Black_nurses_-_J_Lesmond_Jan-Feb2006.pdf

Lurie, Rob, 2022, "A look at the lasting legacy of Canada's first Black doctor, William Wright," February 15.

Mackey, Frank, 2018, "1848, 1861, 1926—Which Came First," *Connections: Journal of the Quebec Family History Society*, vol. 40, no. 3, pp. 7–10, July.

-----, 2020, "Dr. William Wright and Black Enrolment at McGill's Medical School," public lecture, James McGill Society, February 17.

Majors, Monroe Alphus, 1893, "Miss Fredericka Jones, Education," in *Noted Negro Women: Their Triumphs and Activities* (Chicago: Donohoe & Henneberry), http://www.usgenealogyexpress.com/~bhist/bios_1893_notednegrowomen/bios_1893_notednegrowomen_pg_251.htm

Michigan Medicine, 2020, "Pioneers and pathbreakers: Black History milestones in Michigan Medicine," https://www.uofmhealth.org/news/archive/202002/pioneers-and-pathbreakers-black-history-milestones-michigan

Morris, Gayle, 2021, "Native American and Indigenous Nurses You Should Know About," *Nurse Journal*, November 11.

Muskrat Magazine, 2022, "Emily Stowe Scholar Program Summer Student Research Opportunities," February 11.

Nakayama, Don K. 2022, "The Buxton Mission School, the Original 'Pipeline' of Black Surgeons," Part One, *Bulletin of the American College of Surgeons*, March 4.

Payne, Leah and Rachel Oncza, 2017, "Biographical Sketch of Anna H. Jones (1855–1932), *Alexander Street*.

Pompilii, Brittany, 2021, "A Feature on Dr. Sophia B. Jones," *missINFORMED*, March 13.

Reid-Maroney, Nina, 2004, "African Canadian Women of the New World Diaspora (circa 1865)," *Canadian Woman Studies*, vol. 23, no. 2, pp. 92–6.

Rhodes, John, 2021, "Chatham-born doctor helped start nurses' training program in Atlanta, *Chatham-Kent This Week*, March 24.

Rothberg, Emma, 2020-2, "Dr. Rebecca Lee Crumpler," https://www.womenshistory.org/education-resources/biographies/dr-rebecca-lee-crumpler

Ruck, Lindsay, 2017, "Violet King", *The Canadian Encyclopedia*, November 16, updated on January 24, 2019.

Shadd, Adrienne, 1994, 'The Lord seemed to say 'Go': Women and the Underground Railroad Movement, '*We're Rooted Here and They Can't Pull Us Up*', P. Bristow, ed., pp. 41–68.

Shaw, Stephanie J., 1996, *What a Woman Ought to Be and Do: Black Professional Women Workers During the Jim Crow Era* (Chicago: University of Chicago Press).

Slaney, Catherine, 2003, *Family Secrets, Crossing the Colour Line* (Toronto: Dundurn Press).

Smith, Charles, 2004, "Tuition Fee Increases and the History of Racial Exclusion in Canadian Legal Education," Race Policy Dialogue Conference Paper, Ontario Human Rights Commission, December.

Spelman College, 2016, "Sophia B. Jones Charts a Course of Success for African-American Doctors," *Our Stories*, April.

Spelman College, 2020, "Dr. Sophia B. Jones and Ludie Clay Andrews, Class of 1906," *Our Stories*, April.

Steckley, John, 2023, "Sophia Bethena Jones: Canada's First Black Woman to Earn a Medical Degree," October 18, *The Journal of Blacks in Higher Education*.

St-Onge, Josee, 2018, "Edmonton hotel accused of racial discrimination against 4 young men," *CBC News*, November 30.

Stock, Sandra, 2018, "An African Inheritance: Rev. Dr. William Wright, 1827–1918", *Quebec Heritage News*, vol. 12, no. 3, as republished in *Bibliography on English-speaking Quebec*, Brendan O'Donnell, https://quescren.concordia.ca/en/resource/GA83ED4J

Stolp-Smith, Michael, 2018, "Freedmen's Hospital/Howard University Hospital (1862–)," *BlackPast*, March 25.

Sullivan, Nicole, 2022, "Black health-care crusaders; African Canadian pioneers in Nova Scotia nursing history," *Atlantic Canada*, February 8.

Wilberforce University, n.d., "About Wilberforce University," https://wilberforce.edu/about-wilberforce.

Yarhi, Eli, 2013, "Leonard Braithwaite," *The Canadian Encyclopedia*,

Zura, David, 2022, "Toronto City Council to commemorate Canada's first two Black Doctors," *CityNews*, May 18.

CHAPTER FIVE

Sophia's Sisters and Brothers

Sophia had three sisters and two brothers. All of her sisters pursued educational careers and ended up teaching at African American schools. Like Sophia, none of her sisters married or had children. And like her, her sisters also had to leave Canada to achieve their life's goals in the United States. One of Sophia's brothers, George Allen Jones became a carpenter, but as for her other brother, William Alfred Jones, who died in his early twenties, there is a lack of information.

Anna Holland Jones (1855–1932)

Anna Holland Jones was Sophia's older sister, the first born of her siblings. Like the others, she was born in Chatham. Anna too lived a life of hard-won achievement, as an educator, an activist and a writer. She followed the family tradition by graduating from Oberlin College in 1875 at twenty years of age, thirteen years after the first Black woman did. She received a Literary Degree. She received an Honorary Master of Arts in 1892, and in 1893 she was given a Bachelor of Philosophy degree.

From 1885 to 1892, she taught Literature, History and Zoology, and was Dean of Women at Wilberforce University in Ohio, the oldest privately owned African American school in the United States.

From Ohio she moved to Kansas City, Missouri, to teach at Lincoln High School, another learning institution for African Americans. She was the first Black female hired as a teacher in Kansas City. In 1894, an article was written about her in the *Kansas City Messenger*, entitled "A Shame." It was republished in *The Washington Bee*, October 27, 1894, p. 2. The article was about her being offered a better paying teaching job in Washington, D.C., that could take her away from Kansas City.

> A few days ago Miss Anna H. Jones of the Lincoln High School, this city, received a call to be one of the faculty of the Washington D.C. High

School, at a salary much larger than she gets here. As the call comes when Miss Jones has perfected her arrangement here, we do not know whether she will accept it or not, but her going would certainly be a loss to the Kansas City High School, as Miss Jones is better equipped by education and experience than any teacher we have had, or would be able to induce to come. Though a collegiate, being an alumnus of Michigan University, she has never ceased to study and is remarkably well read. However, she is as unassuming as if her attainments were not of a superior order, and does not keep herself on the unapproachable pinnacle that most well-educated people mount. We extend our hearty congratulations to Miss Jones for the honor conferred on her in being called to such a school (https://www.newspapers.com/clip/9247031/anna-h-jones-teacher-in-kansas-city/).

Luckily for the students there and their parents, she did not leave Kansas City to go to Washington.

In 1900, from July 23 to 25, she was one of the American representatives and a speaker at the ground-breaking first Pan-African Conference, held in London, England, one of only two African-American women to be chosen to be so chosen. The title of her paper was "The Preservation of Racial Equality." In 1905, she wrote a two-part essay, "A Century's Progress for the American Colored Woman," in *Voice of the Negro Magazine* (September, pp. 621–3 and October, pp. 692–4).

Anna Jones, 1902

In 1911, she became the first Black principal of the Douglass School in Kansas City, a public school founded in 1890 for the education of African Americans. It was, of course, named after Frederick Douglass (see previous chapter). She remained at this position until her retirement in 1919.

She involved herself politically as well, as a suffragette, campaigning to get her African American sisters the vote and be active politically. She did this through several organizations. In 1893, along with a fellow activist, she established the Kansas City Colored Woman's League in Missouri, and would be their president from 1903 to 1906. This led her to doing such work at the national and international level.

Apart from her own writing, she was written about as well. The African

American writer Katherine Davis Chapman Tilman wrote a poem when she was twenty-one years old, entitled simply "My Queen." It was first published in the *Christian Recorder* of September 10, 1891, and again in *The Works of Katherine Davis Chapman Tillman* (Tate, 1991).

>   My Queen
> To Miss A. H. Jones, lady Principal
>   Wilberforce University
>
> All honor to my dark-eyed Queen,
>   As you rule in your realm of love-
> God keep you from danger dark unseen
>   God guide you with His love.
>
> Pure as a flake of fairest snow
>   Hast thy whole life e'er been-
> Ah, never a nobler one I trow
>   Than thou, my stately queen.
>
> Thou had learned in sorrow's school
>   Some lessons, I know of pain
> Hast let thy heart's deep lava cool
>   And found they cross again.

You can well imagine the amazing positive impact that Anna H. Jones had on the writer, as well as other students who could not put their gratitude into words.

On December 18, 1911, Anna wrote a four-page letter to W. E. B. Du Bois, a prominent African-American scholar and civil rights activist, the first African American to receive a doctorate. He became a professor of history, sociology, and economics at Atlanta University, and was one of the founders of the National Association for the Advancement of

Colored People in 1909. Her letter is summarized as "Describing the discrimination faced by African Americans who have moved into her neighborhood" (https://credo.library.umass.edu/view/full/mums312-b006-i298). She addressed Du Bois as "Dear Friend." She went on to talk about how the 'colored people' who had moved into her neighbourhood were being pressured to leave:

Anna Jones with one of her classes at Lincoln High School

> You will recall our neighborhood when you drove out one day when here, when my sister was here with me. There are 9 homes owned by colored people at the end of the block. The enclosed photos show you the two opposite sides of the street. … The colored people have lived in the houses for periods ranging from 8 years to 2 years. When the 1st colored man purchased in the block there were only 3 white families in the near neighborhood at the other end of the block. New houses were put up near & sold to whites, except the one adjacent to the colored family, which after standing vacant a while was sold to a col. Family & then the other whites gradually sold out & moved away till there were 9 col. In this block, and about 15 in the block to the north of this one.
>
> They lived peacefully till nearly 3 years ago, when the agitation began that some Republican Boss had 'Africanized' the 10th ward.
>
> Meetings were held in a hall denouncing the agents and others who had sold to the col. people and it was said that they had depreciated property etc etc. Feeling ran high and when a place on a neighboring street where no colored had been was sold to a colored man the throwing of dynamite began. After three attacks on this house the colored man moved out and in a few weeks after that they began trying the same methods in our neighborhood on Montgall.
>
> The mayor was approached to send officers in citizen's clothes were stationed at night about the premises. They have been on guard over

a year, but their service has not been efficient enough to prevent the bomb throwing. Up to the last attack the main injury was the breaking of windows, but on the night of the 9th of Nov. last a discharge was set off in the Walden house wrecking it almost completely, so that it is unsafe to live in & could be repaired only at great expense. The house cost originally about $3400. His wife and children were alone in the house, he being in Utah, but fortunately were uninjured, and made their home with a neighbor till they could get quarters in another part of the city. (Jones 1911)

In a front-page article of the Kansas City (Missouri) *Sun* for October 10, 1914, her picture appears first as a fundraiser for a local version of the YWCA,[45] which appears from the pictures and names in the article to be primarily for African American children. The caption along with her pictures tell us that she gave fifty dollars for furnishings, and was a subscriber as well to the building funds.

From August 7 to 10, 1916, she played an important part at the Tenth Biennial Convention of the National Association of Colored Women Program, held in Baltimore. She was one of two members of the Program Committee, as well as being the head of the Education Department.

From 1916 to 1919, she returned to work at Lincoln High School, where she taught English Literature, History and Drawing for the College Preparatory School there. She retired from teaching after that, following forty years an educator, at sixty-four years of age.

Her advocacy for the vote for women, particularly African-American women continued.

The August 1915 edition of *The Crisis*, published by the National Association for the Advancement of Colored People, and the oldest Black-oriented magazine, included "Votes for Women: A Symposium." Anna H. Jones wrote a key article, "Women's Suffrage and Social Reform". In this article she asked:

"[W]hy should a woman "not have the legal means—the ballot—to widen and deepen her work?" Jones argued that if women had the ballot, society as a whole would be improved, and referred to those states in which women had already achieved the right to vote as an example

---

45. The title for the article in the original paper refers to the YMCA, but the online lead uses the title "Anna H. Jones leads YWCA fundraising." This makes more sense.

of the reforms and improvements that would come with women's suffrage (William G. Pomeroy Foundation).

Her fight for women's suffrage must have felt frustratingly slow for her. It was not until 1920, with the passage of the 19th Amendment, that women across the U.S. were finally given the vote. Canadian women received the vote two years earlier. However, it would be some time before the majority of Black women could vote. The 19th Amendment did not eliminate state laws such the poll taxes and literacy tests that operated to keep many African Americans from voting. In some states they still do.

Anna in her later years

She went to live with her sister Sophia in Monrovia, California, where, as mentioned in the previous chapter, the two of them grew oranges commercially. She would do more than just that. In 1921, she founded the Anna H. Jones Women's Club, which offered and still provides financial assistance at various levels of education, especially for area minority high school graduates students intending to go to college.

Their brother George had moved there with his wife and family three years earlier. Anna died on March 7, 1932, and was buried in an unmarked grave in the Live Oak Cemetery in Monrovia. Shortly after her death, the Anna H. Jones Women's Club became affiliated with the National Council of Colored Women's Clubs Inc. In the words of a recent member of the club, with the name of Gwendolyn Jones (it is not known to me whether she belongs to the Anna's family): "In 1932, we organized with the following goals: service to the community, fellowship with women, and to provide financial support to area students bound for college" (Jones 2015).

The club is still involved today with establishing scholarships for young African American women.

Descendants of her family attended the Anna H. Jones Women's Club's 75th Anniversary Benefit Banquet on September 28, 1996.

The house she lived in before her retirement is listed as "Anna H. Jones Residence, 2444 Montgall Avenue" on the African American Heritage Trail of Kansas City, Missouri (https://aahtkc.org/anna-h-jones). Despite this listing, her house is in disrepair and is boarded up.

In 2022, a plaque or marker was erected by the William G. Pomeroy

Foundation in another part of Kansas City. It is part of the National Votes for Women Trail. It reads as follows:

> Anna H. Jones
> Suffragist & Missouri State
> Federation of Colored Women's
> Clubs President Spoke At 1906
> Convention at Second Baptist
> Then at 10th & Charlotte St.[46]

Fredericka Florence Jones (1858–1905)

Fredericka Florence Jones was born in Chatham in 1858, and would spend most of her adult life teaching in a variety of schools in five different states: Florida, Missouri, Ohio, Pennsylvania, and Texas. Like her sisters Sophia and Anna, she was Canada's loss to teaching, and a significant gain for education in the United States.

She early on excelled as a student. In her obituary it was stated that "she was a leader in her classes. She passed the entrance examination at Toronto University[47] and gained exceptional grades at subsequent examinations." She then taught for a year in St. Louis. As noted in the obituary, "When colored teachers were called to teach in St. Louis, Miss Jones and her two sisters responded" (Anonymous, 1905). She then moved to Ann Arbor, Michigan, graduating with a Bachelor of Arts from the University of Michigan in 1887, the same university where her sister Sophia had earned her medical degree two years earlier. Then she went to Wilberforce University in Ohio, presumably to teach alongside her sister Anna. She taught French and German there. As we have seen, her sister Sophia would teach there in later years.

Fredericka seems to have been fragile in health, and needed to live in a warmer climate than that of the northern states and Canada. She went first to Waco, Texas,[48] to teach at what would come to be called Paul Quinn College, the oldest historically Black college in the state (founded in 1872 in Austin, where it was first called the Connectional School for the Education of Negro Youth). It was renamed after the fourth bishop of the African Methodist Episcopal Church, William Paul Quinn (1788–1873), as it was a Methodist

---

46. https://www.wgpfoundation.org/historic-markers/anna-h-jones/
47. That is, the University of Toronto.
48. The school relocated to Waco in 1877.

institute. It provided an academic alternative for African American students (freed slaves and their children) excluded from other post-secondary educational institutions. By 1893 Fredericka was promoted from teacher to become the principal of the school (Majors, 1893:274).

In that year, in a book entitled *Noted Negro Women: Their Triumphs and Activities,* written by Monroe Alphus Majors, Black physician, civil rights leader and author, Fredericka was included as one of three hundred noted women that he wrote about, described with the following complimentary words:

> **MISS JONES** ranks among the leading educators of the race. She is a graduate from the classic halls of the famous Michigan University, Ann Arbor Michigan. And has since done very telling work for our race as teacher in the northern as well as the southern college[s]. She is at present lady principal of Paul Quinn college, Waco, Texas. Her special fitness commends her to the higher educational work among our people, and the above named school has under her watchful care and tutelage, made very great advances in the right direction; She is amiable, most agreeable in manners, and a capable counselor on topics of advanced studies.
>
> Her prominence as well as intellectual ability, entitles her to many pages whereon might be forcibly drawn the illustrious career of one so worthy. We, knowing, **Miss Jones**' love for obscurity, I feel somewhat reluctant in making the fore-going statement, yet by a sense of right we have thus risked our judgment (Majors, 1893:274).

After her work in Waco, Texas, she went to Tallahassee, Florida to teach at the State Normal College for Colored Students, later to become Florida Agricultural and Mechanical College for Negroes, now known as Florida A&M University, the only public historically Black university in the state.

In 1896, she opened in Philadelphia a private school for girls, almost certainly African American girls.[49] As yet, I have learned nothing else about this school. I do not doubt that it offered opportunities for African American girls that were hard for them to find elsewhere. In 1903, she established a similar school in Kansas City, Missouri. According to the anonymous author

---

49. The African-American population in Philadelphia was quite large then, with 32,000 in 1880 and 63,000 a decade and a half later (Wikipedia, "History of Africans in Philadelphia").

of her obituary: "Her success from the very inception of her work secured for her immediate recognition and appreciation, and she was called to the city schools in September, 1904." Unfortunately for the students in the public school where she taught, she would die before the school year was over.

Like her fellow career-driven sisters, Sophia and Anna, Fredericka never married and had no children. However, she did take care of one child. Her obituary makes reference to her "maintaining her little orphan god child, who lost both of its parents within the short space of ten days" (Anonymous, 1905).

That the three sisters remained single should not be surprising, as this was the case with a relatively large number of Black professional women at that time. Stephanie J. Shaw wrote in her illuminating book, *What a Woman Ought to Be and Do: Black Professional Women Workers During the Jim Crow Era*:

> Cognizant of racist and sexist slurs, parents emphasized the importance of disproving the sexual myths and stereotypes and insisted on sexual self-control and, thus again, the demonstration of respectability. Adhering to this code of morality would, however, do more than protect the individual, family and race from embarrassment. A breach of these practices, whether or not it resulted in a premarital or early pregnancy, could easily eliminate the professional opportunities for which the parents were preparing their daughters (Shaw, 1996:24).

A good non-Jones Canadian example of this situation involves Nina Mae Alexander, a Black woman born in Amherstburg, not far from Chatham. Her father, John Henry Mae, was a teacher, as were one of her brothers and a sister. She was admitted to Toronto Normal School in September 1907, after two years of teaching. Nina Mae taught in nearby Rondeau until her retirement. She too, never married, although we learn from her surviving four-month-long diary from 1907, that a good number of men were interested in her and she had to keep them at arms' length to resist their proposals (Bonner, 2014).

Finally, Fredericka's obituary includes a glowing tribute that, although flowery in the style of tributes of that time, should be included here, as she no doubt earned such effusive words of praise.

> None went from her presence without the consciousness of having been in the sunshine of a cultural refined and noble woman. Frail in

statu[r]e, unostentacious [sic] in manner, stalwart in simple Christian character, the influence of her life cannot be said in a day (Anonymous, obituary [of Fredericka Jones], 1905. "An Appreciation," *The Rising Sun,* Kansas City, Missouri, March 17, p. 5).

Although her obituary was published in Kansas, she was buried in the family plot in the Forest Hill Cemetery in Ann Arbor, Michigan.

Emily Priscilla Jones (1862–1951)

We do not know much about Emily Priscilla Jones, only being able to gather a few details from the bits and pieces found on official forms. She was born in Chatham, as her brothers and sisters were, and like her sisters, she did not pursue her teaching career in her native country of Canada. Emily stated in her declaration of naturalization (the process of becoming a U.S. citizen) that she entered the United States, through Detroit, in August, 1882. That is possibly when she enrolled in a teacher training program. In 1902–3, at forty, she was working as a "Matron" at the Manassas Industrial School for Colored Youth, in Manassas, Virginia (Binning, 2008:20). It began operation in 1894, being founded by ex-slave Jennie Dean.

In her thesis written for her master's degree from William and Mary University, Laura Ann Peake wrote that

> The purpose of this school was to offer vocational and academic training to African Americans who had few opportunities for education beyond the elementary level. It was a private school that received a majority of its funding from Northern philanthropists (Peake, 1995).

The 1910 census of Brunswick County, Virginia, had Emily listed as an English teacher. It could be that she taught at the Saint Paul Normal and Industrial School, which began in 1888 as a Black private college affiliated with the Episcopal (Anglican) church. It was located in Brunswick County, unlike the school where she had been a "Matron."

In 1924, at sixty-one, she made what appears to be her first Declaration of Intention to become an American citizen. She described herself as five foot seven and a half inches in height and weighing 190 pounds. She also said that her color was "Black" and her complexion "Dark." In her Declaration of Naturalization of January 30, 1935, she described herself as "brown" in color, with a "light brown" complexion. For "race" she said that she was "African," her nationality "British." And she declared, at seventy-three, that her occupation was "seamstress".

In the 1930 U.S. Census of Monrovia Country, she is recorded as living with her brother George and her sister-in-law Martha as well as with two godsons, Kenneth Chavis and Edwin Thompson. George and Martha had already raised three daughters and two sons of their own. This same household was also recorded in the 1940 U.S. Census, with Emily seventy-eight (and in 1939 made a naturalized American citizen), brother George seventy-six, and sister-in-law Martha seventy.

Emily died on October 1, 1950, at age eighty-eight, as an American citizen, in a hospital in Los Angeles. She was probably buried beside family members in the Live Oak Cemetery in Monrovia.

Sophia's Two Brothers

We know George Allen Monroe Jones (1863–1944) was a carpenter in the building trade, including constructing the family home. He married Martha C. Havenar in 1898. They lived in Monrovia from 1919. He was the only one of his siblings to have children, five of them—Emily, George, Ann, Helen and Jim—who in turn were followed by three more generations to the present. He is buried in the segregated Live Oak cemetery in Monrovia alongside family members.

William

William Alfred Livingstone Jones (1870–1893) was the youngest of the Jones siblings. He may have, like his sister Sophia, gone to the University of Michigan in 1890–1, doing so in the College of Literature, Science and the Arts. It would have been very sad for his siblings that he was the one who died first. On his interment record, it was stated that he died of "consumption [tuberculosis] and bowels." Tuberculosis was a major killer of young and old in those days. He was the first to be buried in what became the family plot in Ann Arbor's Forest Hill Cemetery. His father, James Monroe, and his two sisters, Fredricka and Emily, would later be buried there. On his gravestone were written the moving words: "The one whom we call dead in un-spoken bliss instead lives and loves you."

Conclusions

This stories told in this chapter clearly demonstrate that Sophia was not the only person of her generation in the Jones family to overcome racial restrictions and succeed, even if they had to leave the country of their birth to do so. Again, as noted earlier, it is important to point out that they were exposed to Black role models in their hometown of Chatham that helped them on their path to success.

I would also like to point out that soon after I began researching Sophia's life for a potential article or book, I knew that a discussion of her siblings had to be part of the story.

References

1910 Census of Brunswick County, Virginia, Thirteenth Census of the United States, https://www.archives.com/1940-census/emily-jones-ca-29581021

Anonymous, 2023, "Anna H. Jones (b. 1855–d. 1932), https://kcparks.org/wp-content/uploads/2023/08/Anna-H.-Jones.pdf

Anonymous, 1894, "Anna H. Jones, teacher in Kansas City," "A Shame," https://www.newspapers.com/clip/9247031/anna-h-jones-teacher-in-kansas-city/ (clipped from *The Washington Bee*, October 27, 1894, p. 2).

Anonymous, obituary [of Fredericka Jones], 1905, "An Appreciation," *The Rising Sun,* Kansas City, MO, March 17, p. 5.

Anonymous, 1903, "Sophia B. Jones working at Kansas City," *The Rising Sun,* Kansas City, MO, December 18, https://www.newspapers.com/clip/9264268/sophia-b-jones-working-at-kansas-city/

Anonymous, 1932, "Monrovia News" (Sophia B. Jones obituary), *California Eagle,* Los Angeles, October 7, p. 4.

Anonymous, 1944, "George Allen Jones" (his obituary), *Monrovia Daily News,* March 9, p. 2.

Anonymous, n.d., "Mary Louisa Agar", *Chatham-Kent Physician Tribute,* https://ckphysiciantribute.ca/doctors/mary-louisa-agar/

Anonymous, n.d., "Anna H. Jones," ChangeMakers, https://www.monroviachangemakers.com/anna-jones

Binning, Margaret B., 2008, *Manassas Industrial School Personnel 1894–1938: Faculty, Staff, Students and Graduates; Partial Listing,* Ruth E. Lloyd Information Center (RELIC), Bull Run Library, Manassas, VA.

Bonner, Claudine, 2014, "Nina Mae Alexander: Daughter of Promise," in *The Promised Land,* pp. 91–105, https://doi.org/10.3138/9781442667457-006

Brandice, Nelson, "Paul Quinn College," *Waco History,* accessed May 19, 2022, https://

wacohistory.org/items/show/79

Bristow, Peggy, 1994 " 'Whatever you raise in the ground you can sell it in Chatham': Black Women in Buxton and Chatham 1850-65," *'We're Rooted Here and They Can't Pull Us Up'*, pp. 69–142.

CityNews, 2022, "Canada's First Two Black Doctors—U. of T. Alumni—To Be Honoured with Plaques Near St. George Campus," May 26.

Fryer, Mary B., 1990, *Emily Stowe: Doctor and Suffragist* (Toronto and Oxford: Hannah Institute and Dundurn Press, Canadian Medical Lives, No. 6).

"Fund Raiser," *Kansas City Sun*, Kansas City, MO, October 10, 1914, p. 1.

Gaston, Lois, 2017, "Anna H. Jones: A civil rights activist and educator who inspired the Anna H. Jones Club," *Monrovia's Changemakers: Combatting Bigotry and Segregation*.

Gwiazada, Emily, 2008, "James Barry", *The Canadian Encyclopedia*, January 20, last edited August 17, 2021.

Henry, Natasha, 2021, "Racial Segregation of Black Students in Canadian Schools," *The Canadian Encyclopedia*, August 30.

Howells, Laura, 2017, "New plaque celebrates Albert Jackson, Toronto's first black postman," *Toronto Star*, July 21.

https://www.archives.com/1940-census/emily-jones-ca-29581021

https://www.findagrave.com/memorial/239805320/anna-holland-jones/photo

Jefferies, Keisha, 2020, "Recognizing history of Black nurses a first step to addressing racism and discrimination in nursing, *Dal News*, Dalhousie University, May 13.

Jones, Anna H, 1911, Letter from Anna H. Jones to W. E. Du Bois December 18, 1911, https://credo.library.umass.edu/view/full/mums312-b006-i298

Jones, Sophia B., 1890, "Barrel Trunk," *United States Patent Office*, January 18.

-----, 1912, "Fifty Years of Negro Public Health," *The Annals of the American Academy of Political and Social Science*, pp. 138–46.

Kansas City Heritage Trail, https://aahtkc.org/anna-h-jones

Kennedy, Brendan, 2023, "Canada's first Black doctors honoured with plaques," *Toronto Star*, February 9.

Lesmond, Joan, 2006 "President's View" *Registered Nurse Journal*, https://rnao.ca/sites/rnao-ca/files/Celebrating_Black_nurses_-_J_Lesmond_Jan-Feb2006.pdf

Ling, Susie, 2015, "History of African Americans in Monrovia," https://susieling.wordpress.com/2015/05/22/history-of-african-americans-in-monrovia.

Lurie, Rob, 2022, "A look at the lasting legacy of Canada's first Black doctor, William Wright," CTV News, February 15.

Mackey, Frank, 2018, "1848, 1861, 1926—Which Came First," *Connections: Journal of the Quebec Family History Society*, vol. 40, no. 3, pp. 7–10, July.

-----, 2020, "Dr. William Wright and Black Enrolment at McGill's Medical School," public lecture, James McGill Society, February 17.

Majors, Monroe Alphus, 1893, "Miss Fredericka Jones, Education," in *Noted Negro Women: Their Triumphs and Activities* (Chicago, Donohoe & Henneberry), http://www.usgenealogyexpress.com/~bhist/bios_1893_notednegrowomen/bios_1893_notednegrowomen_pg_251.htm

Michigan Medicine, 2020, "Pioneers and pathbreakers: Black History milestones in Michigan Medicine," https://www.uofmhealth.org/news/archive/202002/pioneers-and-pathbreakers-black-history-milestones-michigan

Morris, Gayle, 2021, "Native American and Indigenous Nurses You Should Know About," *Nurse Journal*, November 11.

Muskrat Magazine, 2022, "Emily Stowe Scholar Program Summer Student Research Opportunities," February 11.

Payne, Leah and Rachel Oncza, 2017, "Biographical Sketch of Anna H. Jones (1855–1932)," *Alexander Street*.

Peake, Laura Ann, 1995, "The Manassas Industrial School for Colored Youth, 1894-1916," Dissertations, Theses, and Masters Projects, William and Mary, Paper 1539625943.

Picture of Anna and her class at Lincoln High School: https://images.squarespace-cdn.com/content/v1/5075895f84ae84c1f4ec0443/1481321784991-RDJIB9ESSCPZWUZM8SCC/jones2.jpg

Ruck, Lindsay, 2017, "Violet King," *The Canadian Encyclopedia*, November 16, updated on January 24, 2019.

Shadd, Adrienne, 1994, " 'The Lord seemed to say 'Go': Women and the Underground Railroad Movement," *'We're Rooted Here and They Can't Pull Us Up'*, P. Bristow, ed., pp. 41–68.

Shaw, Stephanie J., 1996, *What a Woman Ought to Be and Do: Black Professional Women Workers During the Jim Crow Era* (Chicago: University of Chicago Press).

Smith, Charles, 2004, "Tuition Fee Increases and the History of Racial Exclusion in Canadian Legal Education," Race Policy Dialogue Conference Paper, Ontario Human Rights Commission, December.

Spelman College, 2016, "Sophia B. Jones Charts a Course of Success for African-American Doctors," *Our Stories*, April.

Sullivan, Nicole, 2022, "Black health-care crusaders: African Canadian pioneers in Nova Scotia nursing history," *Atlantic Canada*, February 8.

Tate, Claudia, ed., 1991, *The Works of Katherine Davis Chapman Tillman* (Oxford University Press).

United States Census, https://data.census.gov/profile/Brunswick_County,_Virginia?g=050XX00US51025

University of Michigan, General Catalogue of Officers and Students, 1837–1890, p. 80, https://www.google.ca/books/edition/General_Catalogue_of_Officers_and_Students/8nIIAAAAMAAJ?hl=en&gbpv=1&pg=PA57&printsec=frontcove [Fredericka]

Wikipedia, n.d., "Anna H. Jones."

Wikipedia, 2021, "Sophia B. Jones."

William G. Pomeroy Foundation, 2023, https://wgpfoundation.org/historic-marker/anna-h-jones/

https://kcparks.org/wp-content/uploads/2023/08/Anna-H.-Jones.pdf

CHAPTER SIX

Summary and Conclusions

There have been two main goals in writing this book. Telling the stories of Sophia Bethena Jones and her family members was the original intent. An additional goal is providing information about Canada's Black history generally, rooted in the stories of the Joneses, but also important in its own right. There is a lot more to Black history in Canada than I had known or even imagined when I began this project.

For me, and for many of my generation of Canadian scholars of history, anthropology and sociology, Canada's Black history was during our intellectually formative years all but invisible. I remember taking a sociology course on race in my second or third year of university. The professor teaching the course was American (as were many university professors in Canada during the 1960s and 1970s), and, along with my fellow students, I learned a great deal about anti-Black racism in the U.S., but nothing about that same phenomenon in Canada. I cannot precisely remember what I thought about that latter subject at the time, but I can be reasonably sure that I had no awareness of the significant extent to which it existed in Canada's history, and possibly entertained the inaccurate idea that Canada wasn't nearly as anti-Black racist as our neighbour to the south.

As outlined in the first chapter, it was only while working in various projects when I was a college professor teaching sociology and anthropology-based subjects that I began to engage in significant learning on the subject, piece by piece. This was greatly accelerated in the researching and writing of this book, every chapter teaching me more. The most recent such learning came when I began writing this concluding chapter, and came across a statistic that I had never seen before in an article published by Parks Canada in 2020:

> Between c. 1629 and 1834, there were more than 4,000 enslaved people of African descent in the British and French colonies that became

Quebec, Ontario, Nova Scotia, Prince Edward Island, and New Brunswick (Parks Canada, 2020).

On August 1, 1834, the British Parliament passed the Slavery Abolition Act, which prohibited enslavement across most of the British empire. There had been a Canadian move in that direction on July 9, 1793, when the Lieutenant-Governor of Upper Canada, John Graves Simcoe, and his parliament passed the Act to Limit Slavery in Upper Canada. This did not ban slavery, but made illegal what happened to Chloe Cooley. She was an enslaved young woman who was abducted by her slave owner, who wanted to take her to the U.S. to sell her. She physically resisted the act of abduction, which was witnessed by passersby, who would report what they had seen to Lieutenant-Governor Simcoe, influenced him to pass the legislation. While she ended up being sold in New York, and there appears to be nothing known about her subsequent history, her role in influencing the passing of this law has been honoured by a drawing of her on a Canadian stamp issued by Canada Post on January 29, 2023 (Canada Post, 2023). I just learned that on July 1, Canada Day, 2023. I do not post many letters these days, so I was unaware of her picture being on a stamp.

Institutions such as Parks Canada and Canada Post recognizing and telling important stories of our Black history I take to be an encouraging sign. But we still have a long way to go. I am hoping that this book will take some Canadians a few steps along the way, and maybe Sophia B. Jones will finally be recognized as a Canadian role model for those who have to overcome serious obstacles in their lives.

References

Canada Post, 2023, "Black History Month Stamp Honours Chloe Cooley," January 29.

Parks Canada, 2020, "The Enslavement of African People in Canada (c. 1629–1834)," July 31.

-----, 2022, "Government of Canada recognize Chloe Cooley as a person of national historical significance," April 27, 2022.

ACKNOWLEDGEMENTS

Three individuals provided me with a great deal of information, without which this book could not have been written. The first is Samantha Meredith of the the Black Mecca Museum in Chatham, who sent me key sources that got this book off to a strong start, as well as being particularly helpful when my wife Angie and I went to the museum. The second is Ceridwen Ross Collins of the Salt Spring Archives, who provided me with valuable sources, in human and in book form, that enabled me to tell the story of John Craven Jones, one of Sophia's uncles, who established a powerful presence in British Columbia. Closer to home is my Humber College colleague, Sonia Hoy, who was able to find online sources I probably would not have found without her diligent research.

Also to be acknowledged are the two people whose belief in my research and writing helped me greatly in the writing and publishing of this book. David Stover, of Rock's Mills Press, provided me with the publisher I needed for this work, as well as others. Then there is my wife, Angelika Steckley, whose support of my writing enables me to write as much as I do. I could not do it without her.

John Steckley
August 2024

www.ingramcontent.com/pod-product-compliance
Lightning Source LLC
Chambersburg PA
CBHW072212070526
44585CB00015B/1308